RS4L

RECOVERY STRATEGIES 4 LIFE

Student Workbook

Unit 3 (Part A)
Healing From the Past

Developed By:

BLOOM
in the dark

Paula Mosher Wallace
Ginny Priz, CPLC
Evonna Surrette, MA, LPC

Published by Bloom Publishing, an imprint of Bloom In The Dark, Inc.

Recovery Strategies 4 Life Unit 3 (Part A) Student Workbook: Healing From The Past
Paperback edition, Published July 10, 2020

Cover Design: Ginny Priz
Editing: Elizabeth Garrett

ISBN-13: 978-0-9965309-7-2
ISBN-10: 0-9965309-7-5

Bloom-U.org
Bloominthedark.org
RS4L.com

Scripture references are limited quotes from the online versions of these Bibles:
New International Version
King James Version
New King James Version
New Living Translation

Table of Contents

About the Content Developers/Instructors

Paula Mosher Wallace
Ordained Minister

Born in the jungles of Peru to missionary parents, Paula began life saturated in the Word of God. With Bible classes as part of every school year plus 4 years of Bible college, Paula's knowledge of the Truth grew. An Ex-Victim of abuse, Paula became the author and founder of Bloom In The Dark. She also produces and co-hosts Bloom Today, an international TV show discussing abuse. In RS4L, Paula teaches Biblical recovery, highlighting God's heart for healing the broken.

paula@bloominthedark.com | 478-335-3910

Ginny Priz
Certified Professional Life Coach

Being born with her right arm stopping just below the elbow taught Ginny to trust God's plan. But her recovery journey from codependency, alcohol, & panic attacks taught her to trust God with the deep, broken parts of her heart - one moment at a time. To help other women find this freedom, Ginny became a certified Christian life coach, speaker, and author of Ditch The Drama. She also anchors Bloom Today, a Christian talk show broadcast in over 200 countries.

ginny@bloominthedark.com | ginnypriz.com

Evonna Surrette, MA, LPC
Trauma & Attachment Therapist

Evonna's life passion is to provide hope and healing to those who suffer from trauma, attachment, eating, and mood disorders. As an Ex-Victim of trauma and eating disorders, Evonna has extensive professional experience in working with trauma, attachment, and a wide range of mental health issues. Evonna has over a decade in ministry and leadership. Evonna takes a holistic approach (spirit, soul, & body) as she believes in removing the roots, not just treating the symptoms.

refinedhope.com

Introduction

1 Thessalonians 5:23 NKJV
"Now may the God of peace Himself sanctify you completely; and may your
whole spirit, soul, and body be preserved blameless at the coming of our Lord
Jesus Christ."

Welcome to RS4L Unit 3 (Part A)! We are excited to have you continue this program.

In Unit 3 (Part A), we continue to disciple and equip leaders and individuals, who have experienced brokenness, through their healing/recovery journey by applying proven strategies to their lives.

This unit will continue to transform how you see healing/recovery and will equip you with powerful tools to help you heal, so you can effectively help those around you.

Stay on course because at the completion of RS4L Unit 5 you will:

1. Understand that each of us is a triune being made of a spirit, soul, and body, that we can be wounded in all three areas, and healing is needed in all three.
2. Have the ability to identify damaging habits or compulsive behaviors and replace them with positive coping skills.
3. Create and foster meaningful, healthy relationships with others.
4. Surrender your will to God, seek His will, and obey His will on a daily basis.
5. Own your identity in Christ and all that God designed you to be.
6. Develop a healthy support system including a sponsor, accountability partners, recovery support group(s), church, counselor, and/or life coach.
7. Understand how the physical and spiritual realms influence each other on the battlefield of the mind and how to win the battle using a custom-made, detailed plan.
8. Have the knowledge of the impact of spiritual warfare in daily life, understand strategies and tactics of Satan, and how to fight enemy attacks.
9. Be able to identify your needs and practice self-care.
10. Identify where trauma, loss, or stressful events may have wounded you and develop a healthy approach to processing difficult emotions and events.
11. Identify destructive core beliefs and replace them with God's truth.
12. Have the ability to use RS4L materials to lead others through their healing/recovery journey.

Please email us at paula@bloominthedark.com or ginny@bloominthedark.com with any questions, confusion, suggestions, or feedback.

Disclaimer

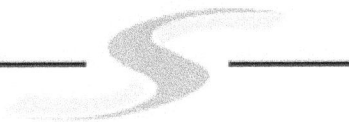

The content, information, opinions, and viewpoints contained in these educational materials are those of the authors or contributors of such materials. The information and content provided on or accessed through Recovery Strategies for Life (Including, without limitations, all print, web materials, and videos) are intended for general informational purposes only.

The information and materials provided on or accessed through the Recovery Strategies for Life program are intended solely for individuals seeking information about healing for the spirit, soul, and body, and are not intended for individuals seeking medical advice or treatment. The instructors and contributors are sharing their personal testimonies of healing. Accordingly, the information and materials presented are not intended nor implied to be a substitute for professional medical advice, diagnosis, or treatment. Any individual always should seek the advice of a physician or other qualified healthcare provider prior to starting any new treatment, selecting a method of treatment, or seeking answers to any questions regarding a medical or mental health condition. Nothing contained or accessed through this program is intended to be and should not be used for medical diagnosis or treatment. Participants and leaders of this program should never disregard professional medical advice, mental health advice, or delay in seeking treatment based on the information contained in this program.

The information and educational material contained herein is meant to promote the general understanding and dialogue of healing spirit, soul, and body. Such information is not meant or intended to serve as a substitute for any healthcare professional's clinical training, experience, or judgment. For participants, such information is not to be a substitute for professional medical, therapeutic, or healthcare advice or counseling. For medical issues or concerns, including decisions about medications and other treatments, participants should always consult their physician or, in serious cases, seek immediate assistance from emergency personnel.

If you are a mental health care professional, you should rely on your professional judgment in evaluating any and all information, and confirm the information contained in this program with other sources and reliable third parties before undertaking any treatment based on it. If you are a consumer or patient, you should evaluate the information together with your physician or another qualified healthcare professional. The instructors and content developers make no warranty that the information contained herein will be error free, and the readers of such information use such at their own risk.

Week 23

Shame OFF You

LISTENING GUIDE

Shame tells us there is something wrong with us, with how we were made, and that flaws cannot be separated from who we are. This is a toxic lie that attacks our identity in Christ. It is not from God.

Instead, the Holy Spirit convicts us of guilt for the purpose of pointing us back to truth, receiving God's love, and coming back into alignment with Him. His motives are not to condemn or berate, but to teach us and encourage us back toward a loving relationship.

We can come to know God's heart better when we understand these truths about shame:

Truth #1: God created us without _____.

> *"And they were both naked, the man and his wife, and <u>were not ashamed.</u>"*
>
> -Genesis 2:25 (KJV)

Not only does God explicitly tell us in Genesis that Adam and Eve were created without shame, but we can look to our own children to see this pattern emerge generation after generation.

NOTES

Babies are not born with shame. They have no concept of shame or self-consciousness until it is learned through their interactions with others in this broken world.

Others can directly speak shame over us or treat us in a manner that evokes shame.

In extreme circumstances, the lie of shame enters through abuse, especially if it occurred in childhood. The wounds from abuse often leave victims with the lie that the abuse was their fault, and they "should" therefore be ashamed of themselves. Sexual abuse of any type can make the shame feel much worse.

This is NOT how God created us in our mothers' wombs! He created us without shame. He made us perfectly according to His plan.

Truth #2: Jesus _____ the shame and dealt with it for us.

God never intended for us to suffer under the weight of shame. Not only did God leave shame out of His original design, but he took on all our shame so we would never have to carry it.

> *"Looking unto Jesus the author and finisher of our faith; who for the joy that was set before him endured the cross, <u>despising the shame</u>, and is set down at the right hand of the throne of God."*
>
> *-Hebrews 12:2 (NKJV)*

God the Father had Jesus's rescue mission planned even before sin and shame entered the world.

Truth #3: We can be _____ shame.

> *"I sought the Lord, and he heard me, and delivered me from all my fears. They looked unto him, and were lightened: and their faces <u>were not ashamed</u>."*
>
> *-Psalm 34:4-5 (KJV)*

Since God created us without shame and then made a way for us to be rescued from shame, we do not have to live with shame at all.

It is a common misconception that living without shame means we will live without humility. This is not true.

Remember, shame tells us there is something innately wrong with us. Under shame we cannot accept that God made us perfectly, let alone that we could ever be reconciled to God.

Humility says it's not about me. Pride says it's all about me. Humility is recognizing we are not God. We need Him to forgive our sins and help us become more like Jesus. With humility, we can accept that we were made perfectly according to God's plan, but we are not able to live in wholeness apart from God.

Reflecting on the fact that we are guilty of sin has a tendency to open the door to shame. That shame can drive us to make destructive choices we might never do under normal circumstances. Lying, cheating, stealing, etc. can suddenly become acceptable behavior when we are desperately trying to protect ourselves. Anything is better than others seeing our shame.

The Bible tells us to combat the shame. We need to remove the leverage shame has by choosing to expose our faults to safe people. Praying for and supporting each other in a safe relationship can help remove the feelings of shame.

> *"Confess your faults one to another, and pray one for another, that ye may be healed. The effectual fervent prayer of a righteous man availeth much."*
>
> -James 5:16 (KJV)

By revealing our struggles, we can allow our sponsors, mentors, and accountability partners to affirm that we are forgiven by God when we repent. Their loving acceptance of us as a person, while condemning the sin, can point us back to God's grace where we will find healing from our shame. The enemy cannot blackmail us with shame when we have no more secrets.

When shame is a lie and not just a feeling, our best attempts to work through stuff to stop feeling shame will not work. Later in this unit, we will identify "the lie of shame" so we can get rid of it.

NOTES

"No Shame" by Moriah Peters

DISCUSSION QUESTIONS
1. Have you ever considered shame to be a lie from the enemy?

2. Are you still harboring shame in secret for something you did or was done to you? If so, why?

3. How does this shame stop you from embracing who God made you to be?

Identifying Shame, Guilt, and Fear Worksheet
Week 23 Homework

Prayer for Binding Shame, Guilt, and Fear

Father God, I come to You with feelings of shame, guilt, and fear. I don't want to admit the broken areas of my past. I'd rather lie to myself and You, but I want healing. Please help me to surrender my shame, guilt, and fear to You at the foot of the cross. Please bring the Truth, as Jesus represented, to the surface. I repent for being in agreement with shame, guilt, and fear. I ask for Your forgiveness. I accept your forgiveness and open myself to Your Truth through the Holy Spirit. In the power of the Holy Spirit, I bind shame, guilt, and fear. You may no longer interfere with my ability to identify and confess the past so I can get free and heal. I choose Truth. In Jesus name, Amen.

Questions:

1. What feelings of shame have blocked you from digging into your past? Describe.

2. What does God say about the shame that has blocked you from digging into your past? List any scriptures that apply.

3. What feelings of guilt have blocked you from digging into your past? Describe.

4. What does God say about the guilt that has blocked you from digging into your past? List any scriptures that apply.

5. What are you afraid will happen if you dig into your past? Describe.

6. What does God say about the fears that have blocked you from digging into your past? List any scriptures that apply.

Exercise

James 5:16 (KJV) "Confess your faults one to another, and pray one for another, that ye may be healed. The effectual fervent prayer of a righteous man availeth much."

Because we want healing, we need to follow God's plan for healing. He says that confessing our sins to each other and praying for each other is part of the healing process. This exercise is the beginning of that process. We are including feelings of shame, guilt, and fear about sins we committed and sins that were committed against us.

Share the answers to 1-6 with a trusted person or persons.

Optional Script:
"Thank you so much for being part of my healing journey. I need to share some things that are connected to feelings of embarrassment and shame. I will need extra prayers, extra support, and extra reminders of truth. I have a tough time being completely honest about my past. I don't need judgment or challenging questions. I just need love, acceptance, and support during this time. Even if you don't understand my story or why I feel like I do, please just show me God's unconditional love. Will you help me?"

If they say yes, then share with them.

Week 24

Discovering the Root

LISTENING GUIDE

Remember, shame and guilt are the tactics the enemy uses to convince us to accept all of his lies. They pull us away from God. The enemy finds it easier to fill us with lies and uses these tactics as proof that we're not good enough to receive God's love and forgiveness. This can rob us of the hope and joy that comes from connection with God.

Recognizing shame and guilt as lies from the enemy will help us not to give into those emotions. We will be able to identify the enemy's tricks faster. This will help us get freedom faster.

We can understand how lies have influenced our past and present circumstances by understanding the following truths:

Truth #1: There is a _____ from cause to consequence in your spirit, soul, and body.

In order to start to identify the roots of the lies, we must first understand how they impact our lives over time.

NOTES

Progression of Damage Chart

Passing of Time →

	Cause	Leads to	Becomes	Consequence
Spirit	Spiritual door point	Lies influence behaviors	Locked into habit of lies	Separation from God
Soul	Lie or thought filter	Belief/viewpoint	Character defect	Damaged relationships
Body	Victimizing event	Unhealthy coping	Addiction	Disease, jail, death

The next two truths reference the Steps to Freedom we discussed in Week 13 (Steps to Freedom) – specifically Steps 1 and 2.

Truth #2: We can _____ the root lie.

The chart above shows the ultimate damage that can result from believing lies. The good news is that we do not have to stay a victim to the lies and just wait for the consequences. At any point in the progression, God has made a way to stop the progression. We can disown the lies, get rid of them, and get back into alignment with God. We start this process by identifying the lie.

When we experience a painful or negative feeling, it's important to take our thoughts captive. When we compare those thoughts to scripture, we can recognize whether it is a truth or a lie. If it's not in alignment with God's truth, it is a lie.

We can also compare the thought or behavior to who God says He is. Then we can compare it to who God says we are. If it is not in alignment with those truths, we know it is a lie.

If there is shame or guilt attached to the thought, the enemy is involved. Remember, being guilty of a sin may be a fact, but the truth is that Jesus took that guilt on the cross. God does not want us to stay stuck in guilt or shame. Repentance and forgiveness are available.

Step 1: Identify

Once we identify the lie, we can start to examine how the lie works. We can discover what the lie sounds like, feels like, and looks like. We can also identify how we act under its influence.

NOTES

Truth #3: Change requires owning our _____ with the lie.

Just because we have believed or experienced consequences of a lie, doesn't mean we consciously chose the lie. Trauma, victimization, or inherited lies are ways it could have been brought into our lives without our conscious choice.

We are not saying that we should ever accept fault for abuse that was done to us. The abuser is always at fault for abuse. There is no way to force an abuser to abuse us.

Step 2: Take Responsibility

Owning our part means taking responsibility for accepting or believing the lie so we can get rid of it. Jesus did not die on the cross so we would be burdened by guilt. Rather, He sacrificed His life so we could identify our participation with sin. Then we can repent and be set free!

WEEKLY WORSHIP
"The Voice of Truth" by Casting Crowns

DISCUSSION QUESTIONS
1. Consider the Progression of Damage chart. Were you surprised to learn how the causes and consequences were related? Why or why not?

2. What consequences have you seen in your life? Can you identify a specific cause in your spirit, soul, and/or body?

3. Are you willing to repent of any lies you've believed to change the trajectory of your future?

Discovering the Root Worksheet

Week 24 Homework

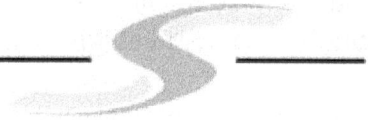

Pick three events from your Life Events Assessment in Week 2 and complete a chart below for each. This will help you discover the roots and effects of that event. If you have more events to work through, you may make as many copies of the one in the appendix as you need for processing purposes.

Life Event #1: _____

Life Event #2: _____

Life Event #3: _____

Life Event #1: _____

	Cause	Leads to	Becomes	Consequence
Body	Victimizing event	Unhealthy coping	Addiction	Disease, jail, death
Soul	Lie or thought filter	Belief/viewpoint	Character defect	Damaged relation-ships
Spirit	Spiritual door point	Lies influence behav-iors	Locked into habit of lies	Separation from God

Life Event #2: _____

	Cause	Leads to	Becomes	Consequence
Body	Victimizing event	Unhealthy coping	Addiction	Disease, jail, death
Soul	Lie or thought filter	Belief/viewpoint	Character defect	Damaged relationships
Spirit	Spiritual door point	Lies influence behaviors	Locked into habit of lies	Separation from God

Life Event #3: _____

	Cause	Leads to	Becomes	Consequence
Body	Victimizing event	Unhealthy coping	Addiction	Disease, jail, death
Soul	Lie or thought filter	Belief/viewpoint	Character defect	Damaged relation-ships
Spirit	Spiritual door point	Lies influence behav-iors	Locked into habit of lies	Separation from God

Week 25

Eliminating the Root

LISTENING GUIDE

Now that we know how to better identify the root of the lies, we can take a closer look at the process of eliminating those roots.

It all goes back to the Steps to Freedom we discussed in Week 13 (Steps to Freedom) – specifically Steps 3, 4, and 5.

Step to Freedom #3: Repent for agreeing with the lie and committing the sin.

In this step, we can pray and repent for our sins and the sins of our past generations (i.e. iniquities)

Nehemiah 9:2 (KJV) "And the seed of Israel separated themselves from all strangers, and stood and confessed their sins, and the iniquities of their fathers."

Deuteronomy 5:9-10 (NIV) "You shall not bow down to them or worship them; for I, the Lord your God, am a jealous God, punishing the children for the sin of the parents to the third and fourth generation of those who hate me, but showing love to a thousand generations of those who love me and keep my commandments."

Numbers 14:18 (KJV) "The LORD [is] longsuffering, and of great mercy, forgiving iniquity and transgression, and by no means clearing [the guilty], visiting the iniquity of the fathers upon the children unto the third and fourth [generation]."

NOTES

Paying lip service with this kind of prayer will be ineffective. It's not about saying the right words to meet performance qualifications. Repentance is a heart change and a head change.

We surrender our thoughts and feelings to God and accept His thoughts and feelings – even if we don't fully agree or understand. As a result, repentance includes stopping the behavior and replacing it with the actions that are aligned with Christ.

Ezekiel 14:6 (KJV) "Therefore say unto the house of Israel, Thus saith the Lord God; Repent, and turn yourselves from your idols; and turn away your faces from all your abominations."

Step 3: Repent for Participating in the Lie

Accept God's forgiveness that was already paid for on the cross. Remember, repentance is not about taking on guilt or shame, but making a change because of the Holy Spirit's conviction.

Step to Freedom #4: Disown the lie.

As you pray, speak out loud your disagreement with the lie. Having your spirit, soul, and body in alignment adds power to your choices. Rejecting the lie on all levels gives you leverage to get rid of the lie so you can heal.

Proverbs 18:21 a (KJV) "Death and life are in the power of the tongue."

2 Corinthians 4:2 (KJV) "But have renounced the hidden things of dishonesty, not walking in craftiness, nor handling the word of God deceitfully; but by manifestation of the truth commending ourselves to every man's conscience in the sight of God."

Step 4: Disown the Lie

By disowning it, we can come out of agreement with the lie and enter into agreement with God. After all, nothing we can do will break the curse of sin. Only the power of Christ, who already broke the curses, will break the chains of sin so we can be free.

Galatians 3:13 (KJV) "Christ hath redeemed us from the curse of the law, being made a curse for us: for it is written, Cursed [is] everyone that hangeth on a tree."

Step to Freedom #5: Get rid of the lie

Prayer is still our most important action. We can take authority over the lie, *in the name of Jesus* and *by the blood of Jesus*. The ONLY power we have is *through the power of the Holy Spirit*.

Through the Holy Spirit's power, we can bind the lie and tell it to leave silently without causing any more damage. Lies enter silently so we know they can leave silently.

Matthew 16:19 (KJV) "And I will give unto thee the keys of the kingdom of heaven: and *whatsoever thou shalt bind on earth shall be bound in heaven: and whatsoever thou shalt loose on earth shall be loosed in heaven."*

Step 5: Get Rid of the Lie

Tell the lie that it has no rights to your life because you have repented and disowned it. Then, tell the lie to leave you alone and go where God designated ("dry places" or "hell").

Luke 11:24 (KJV) "When the unclean spirit is gone out of a man, he walketh through *dry places,* seeking rest; and finding none, he saith, I will return unto my house whence I came out."

Don't leave yourself empty and vulnerable after you get rid of the lie. Ask God to fill the empty space with the fullness of the Holy Spirit!

Ask God to bring healing into any place where there has been damage because of the lie. Ask God for healing from wounds in your spirit, soul, and body. If you know of specific damage that has been done, or are struggling with illness, cravings, or thought patterns, ask for healing in those specific areas.

God has a heart for healing. He wants you to function according to His design and not stay bogged down in damage from the enemy's lies.

James 4:2 (NKJV) "…You do not have because you do not ask."

Unfortunately, God may not heal everything we want. Creative miracles and healing are always possible with God, but He does not heal just because we think we can "earn" it through faith or performance.

God looks at what is good for our eternal best, and He gives us what will bring us eternal life and glorify Him. Continue asking God for healing and freedom. Then trust Him to give you His eternal best.

NOTES

WEEKLY WORSHIP
"Waging War" by Cece Winans

DISCUSSION QUESTIONS

1. What sin(s) have you regretted, but haven't actually repented or changed your choices?

2. Do you have a personality trait or habit that you've always hated? What is it? How would it feel to disown it and no longer act that way?

3. If you could immediately get rid of a lie that you used to think "that's just how I am," what lie would it be? How would you feel without it?

Full Family Tree Worksheet
Week 25 Homework

In this exercise you will draw a diagram of your family tree that includes the physical, mental, and spiritual health of each person. Use the previous family trees created in Weeks 5, 10, and 22 to complete this combined family tree. Ask the Holy Spirit to help you remember and include all important information.

To give you enough room, there is a full page provided for each of your parents' families. There is also a sample family tree provided to give you some inspiration. You do not need to include boxes for any category of family member that is not in your family (for example, you do not need a box for cousins, if you do not have any cousins).

If you have children and grandchildren, you may include them on either family tree. You are not required to write them twice, but you may wish to do so if you want to see the correlation to each parent's family.

If there are too many words to fit in a small space, use the letters, numbers, and Roman numerals to represent—A, 4, xiii, etc.

Sin Patterns	Mental Health Patterns	Physical Health Patterns
A. Cultural influences	1.	i.
B. Passiveness, inaction	2.	ii.
C. Fear, stress, or anxiety	3.	iii.
D. Envy, jealousy	4.	iv.
E. Anger, hatred	5.	v.
F. Bitterness or un-forgive-ness	6.	vi.
G. Blame toward others	7.	vii.
H. Rejection of others	8.	viii.

I. Unable to accept love from others	9.	ix.
J. Victim mentality	10.	x.
K. Cravings, obsessions, or fetishes	11.	xi.
L. Addictions	12.	xii.
M. Pride or narcissism	13.	xiii.
N. Blame toward self	14.	xiv.
O. Rejection of self	15.	xv.
P.	16.	xvi.
Q.	17.	xvii.
R.	18.	xviii.
S.	19.	xix.
T.	20.	xx.

Full Family Tree (Sample)
Mother's Side

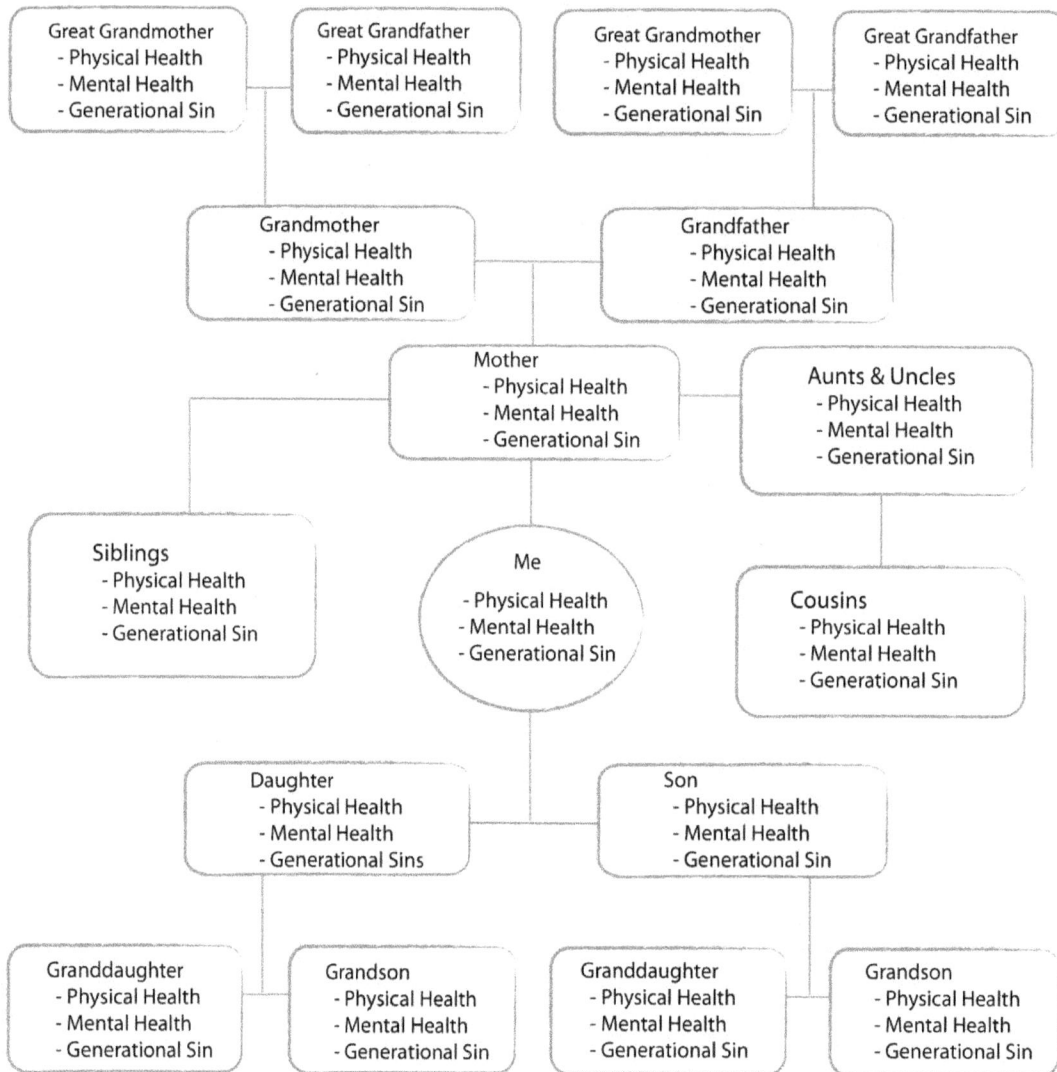

Great Grandmother
- Physical Health
- Mental Health
- Generational Sin

Great Grandfather
- Physical Health
- Mental Health
- Generational Sin

Great Grandmother
- Physical Health
- Mental Health
- Generational Sin

Great Grandfather
- Physical Health
- Mental Health
- Generational Sin

Grandmother
- Physical Health
- Mental Health
- Generational Sin

Grandfather
- Physical Health
- Mental Health
- Generational Sin

Mother
- Physical Health
- Mental Health
- Generational Sin

Aunts & Uncles
- Physical Health
- Mental Health
- Generational Sin

Siblings
- Physical Health
- Mental Health
- Generational Sin

Me
- Physical Health
- Mental Health
- Generational Sin

Cousins
- Physical Health
- Mental Health
- Generational Sin

Daughter
- Physical Health
- Mental Health
- Generational Sins

Son
- Physical Health
- Mental Health
- Generational Sin

Granddaughter
- Physical Health
- Mental Health
- Generational Sin

Grandson
- Physical Health
- Mental Health
- Generational Sin

Granddaughter
- Physical Health
- Mental Health
- Generational Sin

Grandson
- Physical Health
- Mental Health
- Generational Sin

Full Family Tree
Father's Side

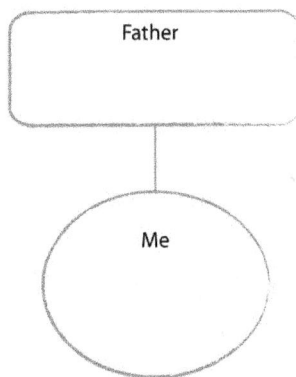

Father

Me

Full Family Tree
Mother's Side

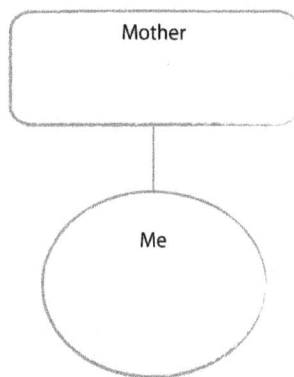

Mother

Me

Identifying Inherited Patterns Worksheet
Week 25 Homework

The purpose of this exercise is to understand what you inherited that you want to change. Don't include the issues from the family tree that you don't believe have impacted your spirit, soul, or body. This is a personal journey. Ask the Holy Spirit to help you see and understand so you can get every ounce of healing available to you.

Look at your combined family tree. Make a list of all the areas of sin patterns, mental and physical damage or dysfunction you inherited below.

1. Generational Sin Patterns (lust, lying, stealing, gossiping, worry, violence, control, anger, etc.)

2. Mental Health Patterns (mental diagnoses, conditions, trauma, symptoms, and/or addictions):

3. Physical Health Patterns (conditions, illnesses, and/or addictions):

Week 26

Diving Deep

This week we are diving deeper into the concepts from Week 16 (Trauma Points & Symptoms). Please review for added clarity.

No matter what our experience with trauma, we can work toward healing by utilizing these three strategies:

Strategy #34

Identifying _____

Triggers are external events or circumstances that may produce very uncomfortable emotional or psychiatric symptoms. Examples include: anxiety, panic, discouragement, despair, or negative self-talk.

Having knee-jerk reactions to triggers is normal. These can be anything from experiencing intense emotions to experiencing flashbacks that transport you back to the original trauma.

NOTES

Triggers can even shift our responses and feelings to a much younger developmental age than we would be normally. A forty-year-old might respond as a young child or a teenager in response to a specific trigger. This usually happens when the trigger is to a trauma that first happened when we were young and still developing. Trauma can stunt our development in an area. Healing can help us "grow up" in that developmental area.

Triggers are very personal. Different things trigger different people. If we don't recognize them and respond to them appropriately, we can get sucked into a downward destructive spiral.

If we can identify our triggers, we can be prepared to use our healthy coping mechanisms. We can learn new responses to those triggers as we heal. "Every trauma trigger is an opportunity to heal" when we run to God and use our tools. Eventually, the triggers will not be able to cause that harm anymore.

Clusters

Experiencing triggers can be a messy process. Unfortunately, it gets even messier when we come across a trigger cluster.

Clusters arise when multiple triggers occur at the same time or in rapid succession.

For example, if Jane is triggered by small spaces, older men, and organized religion, she will likely experience a cluster if she is approached by an older man in a church meeting held in a small room.

Our response to a cluster is more intense than it would be to a single trigger. Confusion and lies seem magnified and overwhelming.

In such an intense triggered state, we can relapse into old, unhealthy coping skills without consciously choosing them. We may experience mild to extreme dissociation. As always, getting grounded is the number one priority.

Because there are multiple triggers, it can take additional time, energy, and processing to identify the lies, where they came from, and how they affected us. This is a normal response and is not an indication that we have gone backward in our healing.

Trigger clusters are a result of trauma and are nothing to be ashamed of. By using our strategies and tools, we can leverage clusters to help us identify lies and process new areas of healing.

With practice, we can become more adept at identifying triggers and processing our thoughts and emotions in a healthy way. Over time, we will continually diminish the intensity of the trigger, the time it takes to process, and the impact it has on our life.

When the trauma is fully processed and healed, the trigger will cease to be a trigger anymore.

NOTES

Strategy #35

Identifying _____

Flashbacks are the sudden and unexpected re-experiencing of a past trauma or the elements of past traumatic events. We may see the original trauma like a virtual reality video we're caught up in. The emotions that arise by re-experiencing the trauma are usually intense.

Flashbacks can be visual or just emotional. Emotional flashbacks feel like the emotional response to the original trauma as if it were still happening. Because emotional flashbacks may not have any direct memories attached, they can be more difficult to identify and process. If we go from 0 to 60 emotionally in an instant, that signifies it's an emotional flashback. Then we can ask the Holy Spirit to bring to mind the originating trauma so we can begin to address it.

Flashbacks can recur years after the initial trauma and will continue until we process the trauma. We can start to do this by working with a counselor or sharing with a trusted, safe person. We can tell them what happened to us and allow ourselves to begin feeling the emotions that arise.

As we process the trauma, visual flashbacks will transition into memories that pop up involuntarily, and then eventually become voluntary memories.

Time alone does not heal this kind of wound. People do not simply "grow out of it." We have to be intentional about this part of healing.

Healing is possible, but only through processing the feelings and facts of the original trauma. We need to integrate those experiences with a healthy perspective as part of our current lives. Stuffing, avoiding, and denying flashbacks will not help and may intensify their effects.

If you are experiencing flashbacks, give yourself grace. It does not mean you are more broken. It does mean you are ready and able to heal. Shaming yourself (or others) for experiencing flashbacks will only slow down the healing process. Choose grace and move forward in the messy and usually frustrating healing process.

NOTES

Strategy #36

Identifying _____

Most people who have experienced trauma also experience some level of dissociation.

Signs and symptoms of **dissociation** may include:
- A sense of being detached from yourself and your emotions
- A perception of the people and things around you as distorted and unreal
- A blurred sense of identity
- Significant stress or problems in your relationships, work, or other important areas of your life
- Inability to cope well with emotional or professional stress
- Mental health problems, such as depression, anxiety, and suicidal thoughts and behaviors
- Memory loss (amnesia) of certain time periods, events, people, and information

There are several levels of severity when it comes to dissociating. From least to greatest they are Emotional Numbing, Depersonalization, Derealization, Amnesia, Identity Confusion, and Identity Separation.

Emotional Numbing is the least severe form of dissociation. Most of us have tried to escape through this kind of behavior at one time or another. Examples include:
- Binge watching TV or movies
- Binge reading books
- Gaming
- Social media
- Extreme exercise
- Excessive sleep
- Workaholism

Depersonalization symptoms include:
- A sense that you're an outside observer of your body, thoughts, or emotions
- Feeling as if you were floating in air above yourself
- Feeling like a robot or that you're not in control of your speech or movements
- The sense that your body, legs, or arms appear distorted, enlarged, or shrunken
- The sense that your head is wrapped in cotton or floating like a balloon
- A sense of emotional or physical numbness
- A sense of numbness to the events and world around you
- A sense that your memories lack emotion
- A sense that your memories actually happened to someone else

NOTES

Derealization symptoms include:
- Feelings of being alienated from or unfamiliar with your surroundings — for example, like you're living in a movie or a dream
- Feeling emotionally disconnected from people you care about, as if you were separated by a glass wall
- Surroundings that appear distorted, blurry, colorless, two-dimensional, or artificial
- A heightened awareness and clarity of your surroundings
- Distortions in perception of time, such as recent events feeling like distant past
- Distortions of distance and the size and shape of objects

Amnesia's primary symptom:
- The sudden inability to remember past experiences or information

Identity Confusion symptoms include:
- Feelings of confusion about your personality, likes and dislikes, dreams and values
- Inability to remember who you are or who you have been

Identity Separation is referred to as Dissociative Identity Disorder (DID). Secular counseling standards describes DID as multiple parts of one's personality being expressed separately as different identities rather than one integrated sense of self. They believe this is the brain's way of protecting itself from processing repeated, severe childhood trauma.

Psychology alone does not account for the spiritual influences like lies that can enter through trauma, and in extreme cases of trauma, take over.

If you have any of the following symptoms, you may be experiencing this without having identified it previously:
- Loss of time and memory
- A major change in personality that is out of your control
- Watching yourself behave in ways that are totally different than you want
- Feeling like someone else is using your body
- If you have sudden urges to be a different gender, use a different name, or dress in completely different types of clothing
- Times when your tastes, desires, and behaviors are completely different than your normal
- Others commenting about you not being yourself
- Others describing your behavior during times you can't remember in conjunction with one or more symptoms above.
- "Dr. Jekyll/Mr. Hyde" types of discrepancies

NOTES

WARNING: See a doctor if you have feelings of Depersonalization, Derealization, Amnesia, Identity Confusion, or Identity Separation that:
- **Are disturbing you or are emotionally disruptive**
- **Don't go away or keep coming back**
- **Interfere with work, relationships, or daily activities**

If someone you know is struggling with these symptoms, encourage them that hope is real, and they are not alone. Healing is possible! Then recommend that they seek professional help as soon as possible as they move forward in their healing journey.

If you would like more information about the spiritual issues related to Identity Separation, contact us at paula@bloominthedark.com or ginny@bloominthedark.com

WEEKLY WORSHIP
"Way Maker" by Michael W. Smith

DISCUSSION QUESTIONS
1. How does understanding triggers, flashbacks, and dissociation shed light on your experiences (whether those are personal experiences or your interactions with individuals who experience these firsthand)?

2. Triggers, flashbacks and dissociation are wounds left by the enemy. How can this understanding help you have patience and grace for yourself and others who are healing?

3. Strategy #9 tells us that God can restore as if never broken. What's interfering with your ability to believe that God can restore these trauma wounds as if they were never there?

Identifying Trauma & Triggers Worksheet
Week 26 Homework

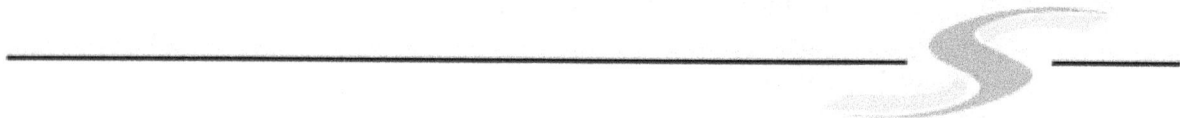

In the space below, write yourself a letter expressing love for who you are and how far you've come. Tell yourself that you are giving yourself grace for this healing process and loving yourself through it.

Before filling out the chart below, get into a safe place where you will not be interrupted or disturbed. Have your list of promises handy and ready to fight lies or triggers if they arise.

Trigger/Trauma	Intensity (1-10)	Response or Feelings	Truth that stabilizes
Getting yelled at	7	fear, shame, hiding	"I am not responsible for other's reactions. I do not deserve to get yelled at. I don't need to be afraid."

Week 27

Uncover

LISTENING GUIDE

Over the next eleven weeks, we'll be taking a closer look at some specific lies the enemy has used for thousands of years to keep God's children in bondage.

Specifically, we'll be examining the following attributes for each group of lies:

- What they sound like in our thoughts
- What they feel like in our emotions
- What they look like in our spiritual lives
- How they show up in our physical being or actions

Examining how these lies work will allow us to identify how they've impacted our lives and help us to get rid of them!

Remember, the enemy is crafty! He may try to tempt you with each lie as we examine it. For example, some of us have struggled with more feelings of anger during the week we identify and dig out the roots of anger.

These temptations are not failures. Rather, these temptations are signs we are in a spiritual battle. The enemy would not try to attack us if he didn't see us as a threat. The temptations reveal that the enemy is actually worried about us gaining more freedom. See it as a compliment. Just don't agree with guilt, shame, or fear over this.

NOTES

When temptations (or triggers) arise in the form of thoughts, emotions, or circumstances, see it as an opportunity. Pay attention to how the lies want to control you or pull you away from God. When they show up, they also reveal how they work. This will help you identify the lies more easily.

You may be able to quickly identify and dig out some lies. You'll have to process and dig out other lies after having some time and distance from the temptation or trigger. These variations are normal. Our processing is different because our experiences and wounds are different.

Thank God the solution is consistent. Jesus is the same yesterday, today, and tomorrow. He gives us the opportunity to repent, accept God's love, and get rid of these lies!

There are a few recovery concepts you'll want to keep at the forefront of your mind as you walk through this process. Because you will be directly addressing the lies that want to cause sin and death, it's important to be prepared before uncovering them.

Concept #1: Utilize your healthy _____.

Having your support team in place before you start will make this process infinitely easier. This process will take up more emotional, mental, and physical bandwidth. Trying to gather a support team in the middle of this process would be much more difficult for everyone.

You'll want to lessen the torment caused by these enemy lies. Sharing temptations and feelings as they arise will lessen their power over you. The longer you keep anything bottled up, the more time the enemy will have to torment you.

Let your support system know you'll be going through this process of getting rid of lies now. Ask them to be a little more discerning and inquisitive about your journey. Give them permission to call out any behavior, words, or beliefs that align with the lies you're working on.

Make sure to have the Comprehensive Action Plan & Self-Care Guide handy! Share your action plan and plan your self-care for the coming weeks. Go ahead and schedule self-care with friends or partners a few weeks out to keep your spirits up. This is an intense process so plan for ways to decompress and have fun to give your life healthy balance.

Concept #2: Utilize your _____.

We've highlighted a few of the strategies we think you'll need most often when fighting enemy lies. During the next week, read through the listening guides. Focus on the lessons with these strategies. Review any notes you made for your specific journey.

- #1 - Be Honest with Yourself (Week 1)
- #6 - Grace for Realistic Recovery (Week 3)
- #10 - Putting on the Armor of God (Week 7)
- #19 - Emotional Detox (Week 11)
- #24 - Recognizing and Replacing Lies (Week 17)
- #25 - Eternal Perspective (Week 18)

NOTES

If you have experienced trauma and/or have been diagnosed with PTS/PTSD/CPSD, it's critical you review the following strategies as well:

- #32 - Grounding (Week 21)
- #33 - Processing (Week 21)
- #34 - Identifying Triggers (Week 26)
- #35 - Identifying Flashbacks (Week 26)
- #36 - Identifying Dissociation (Week 26)

Concept #3: Utilize your _____.

First, we recommend keeping your Bible handy, as God's word is a powerful, living message that the Holy Spirit can use to guide you.

Next, keep your RS4L workbooks handy! There are tons of resources in these workbooks that are available to remind you of truth no matter what your feelings or circumstances may be.

- Cognitive Distortions (Week 10)
- God's Voice vs. Enemy Voice (Week 12)
- Steps to Freedom (Week 13)
- Stages of Grief (Week 14)

Finally, what do you have already at your disposal to remind you of the truth? Do you have books, articles, recovery literature, or Bible studies that can remind you of nuggets of truth?

Concept #4: Utilize your _____.

You've already created many tools through the worksheets and exercises in this study. By filling them out, you have customized them to your story.

Looking back at what you've written will help remind you of the journey you're on. This will provide context to counteract strong feelings (or lies) that may want to overwhelm you during this process.

- Life Events Assessment (Week 2)
- Comprehensive Action Plan (Week 8)
- Emotional Survival Kit (Week 8)
- Self Care Guide (Week 8)
- Taking Thoughts Captive Worksheet (Week 9)
- Relational Diagram (Week 11)
- Where Do You Feel the Pain? Worksheet (Week 15)
- List of Baby Steps (Week 16)
- Identity in God Worksheet (Week 17)
- Spiritual Gifts Test (Week 18)
- Creating Stabilization Worksheet (Week 21)
- Family Tree (Week 25)
- Identifying Trauma & Triggers Worksheet (Week 27)

NOTES

No matter what challenges or feelings arise, God will never leave us nor forsake us—ever! We can be sure He is working all things for our good.

Father God's heart is for healing. We can rest under His wing and seek refuge at every moment. Even when we may face temptation, confusion, or overwhelming emotions, we can be sure God is leading us to greater healing and freedom! Above all, trust God!

If you need a reminder of God's help, read Psalm 91.

WEEKLY WORSHIP
"Believer" by Rhett Walker

DISCUSSION QUESTIONS

1. What three strategies have been the most helpful in your journey so far?

2. What tools have been the most helpful for you in identifying lies so far?

3. Who is your strongest safe support person right now? Why?

Review & Reach Out to Support System
Week 27 Homework

James 5:16 (NIV) "Therefore confess your sins to each other and pray for each other so that you may be healed. The prayer of a righteous person is powerful and effective."

Reach out to your support system:

Optional Script:
"Thank you so much for being part of my healing journey. In the next three months, I will be addressing the spiritual roots of a lot of the damage in my life and family of origin. This will be an intense time of getting rid of lies that have trapped me in the damage of my past. Would you be willing to walk this part of my journey with me? The enemy doesn't like losing ground, so stuff will get more intense as I kick his lies out of my life. I will need extra prayers, extra support, and extra reminders of truth. I may need to share stuff from my past that will be tough to be honest about. I don't need judgment or challenging questions. I just need love, acceptance, and support during this time. Even if you don't understand the process, please just show me God's unconditional love. Can you commit to helping me?"

Name: _____ Name: _____
Role: _____ Role: _____
Date Contacted: _____ Date Contacted: _____

Name: _____ Name: _____
Role: _____ Role: _____
Date Contacted: _____ Date Contacted: _____

Name: _____ Name: _____
Role: _____ Role: _____
Date Contacted: _____ Date Contacted: _____

Name: _____ Name: _____
Role: _____ Role: _____
Date Contacted: _____ Date Contacted: _____

Name: _____ Name: _____
Role: _____ Role: _____
Date Contacted: _____ Date Contacted: _____

Name: _____ Name: _____
Role: _____ Role: _____
Date Contacted: _____ Date Contacted: _____

Review Your Strategies:
- #1 - Be Honest with Yourself (Week 1)
- #6 - Grace for Realistic Recovery (Week 3)
- #10 - Putting on the Armor of God (Week 7)
- #19 - Emotional Detox (Week 11)
- #24 - Recognizing and Replacing Lies (Week 17)
- #25 - Eternal Perspective (Week 18)
- #32 - Grounding (Week 21)
- #33 - Processing (Week 21)
- #34 - Identifying Triggers (Week 26)
- #35 - Identifying Flashbacks (Week 26)
- #36 - Identifying Dissociation (Week 26)

Review Your Resources:
- Cognitive Distortions (Week 10)
- God's Voice vs. Enemy Voice (Week 12)
- Steps to Freedom (Week 13)
- Stages of Grief (Week 14)

Review Your Tools:
- Life Events Assessment (Week 2)
- Comprehensive Action Plan (Week 8)
- Emotional Survival Kit (Week 8)
- Self Care Guide (Week 8)
- Taking Thoughts Captive Worksheet (Week 9)
- Relational Diagram (Week 11)
- Where Do You Feel the Pain? Worksheet (Week 15)
- List of Baby Steps (Week 16)
- Identity in God Worksheet (Week 17)
- Spiritual Gifts Test (Week 18)
- Creating Stabilization Worksheet (Week 21)
- Family Tree (Week 25)
- Identifying Trauma & Triggers Worksheet (Week 27)

Preview of the Freedom Process
Week 27 Homework

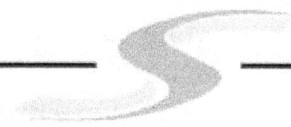

Peeling the Onion

Consider the image of the spiral below. Notice how the lies get closer and closer to the center. There are layers, similar to an onion. The lies on the outside of the spiral have more surface impact on our lives. But as we get closer to the center, the lies begin to affect us more and more deeply. The lies in our minds can be louder and seem more important. The feelings we experience as a result of these lies get more and more intense as we press on.

We start on the outside of the spiral for two reasons: first, because these are the easiest to uncover and eliminate and, second, because you'll need to build your identifying skills before you can tackle the more deeply set lies. Each layer of freedom empowers you to face the next layer.

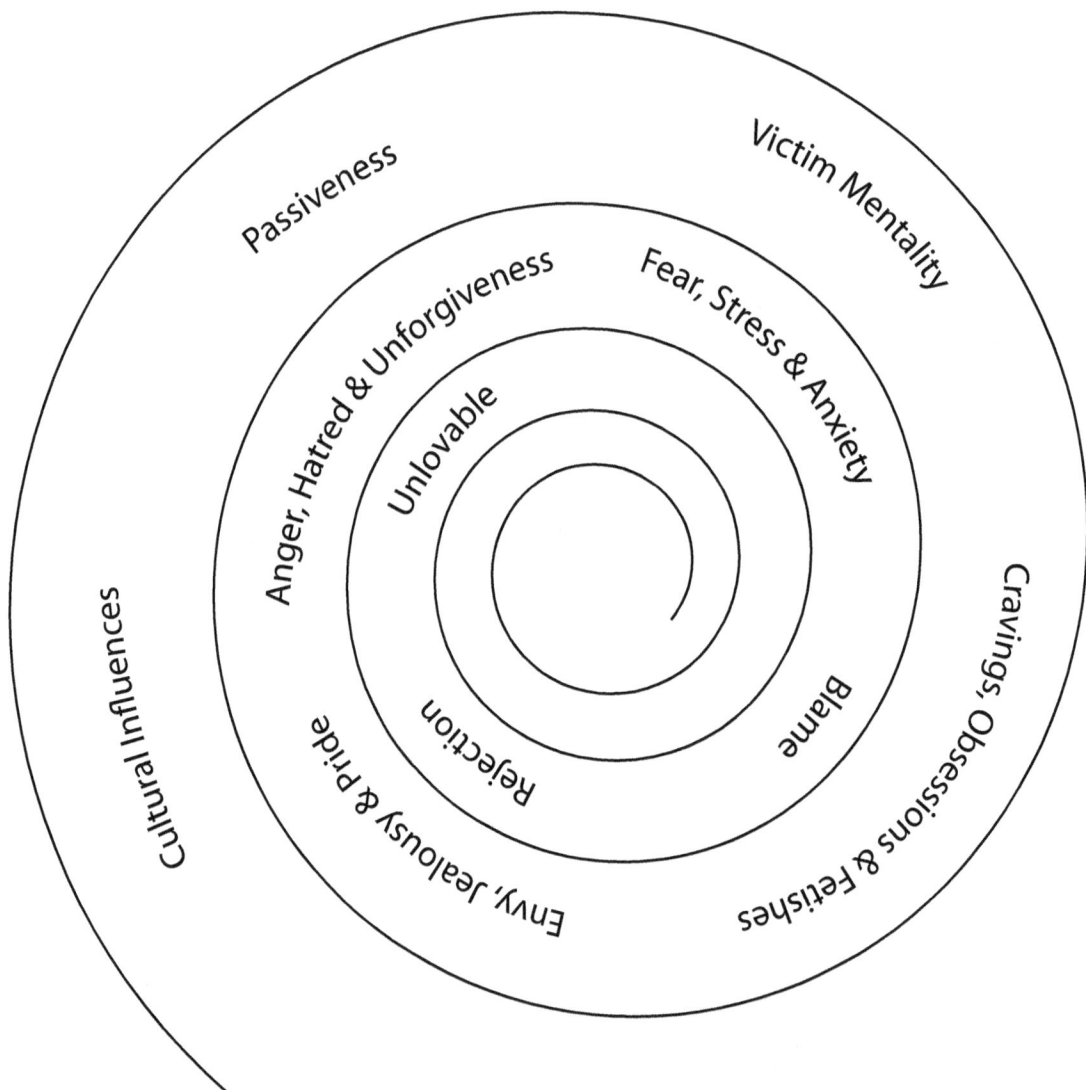

As you address each lie, it is possible that the lies that came before will try to tempt you again. For example, as you address envy, you may also be tempted to obsess about always being a victim or relapse on an addiction.

The enemy tailors these temptations for maximum impact. This is why you must build your ability to be vigilant and take your thoughts captive.

Ladies (sorry guys), be aware that the enemy can try to take advantage of the hormones released during your monthly cycle. You may be hypersensitive and more susceptible to a variety of lies.

CAUTION:
It is EXTREMELY important that these lies are addressed in this order. DO NOT move ahead in the workbook and attempt to address these lies out of order. Watch the videos and do the homework in order. Going in order ensures that you will have the knowledge, skills, and muscles needed to address the next lie, and then the next, and so on.

Trying to deal with a lie when you are not fully equipped may lead to excess confusion, unnecessary triggers, spiraling emotions, or poor decision making.

If you have a history of suicidal thoughts or ideations, please go through this process with your safest accountability/support person with you or within easy reach. Be honest with them about your thoughts and temptations. Please ask as many people as possible to be praying for you.

Ephesians 6:12 (KJV) For we wrestle not against flesh and blood, but against principalities, against powers, against the rulers of the darkness of this world, against spiritual wickedness in high places.

Helplines are listed in the appendix as well.

Tips to Recognize the Strategies of the Enemy

The enemy wants to distract you from working to take back ground. Do not be afraid. The best defense against these strategies is to keep moving forward. The enemy doesn't get to win.

Possible distractions:
- Things going wrong
- Emotional tailspins, intense emotions
- Distractions
- Anxiety or depression
- Exhaustion, tiredness, lack of energy
- Accusations or getting blamed
- Confusion or difficulty focusing
- Anger or rebellion against the process
- Not being in "the mood" to move forward with this process
- Fear that you'll do this wrong or it won't help
- Deflecting to other's issues instead of dealing with your own

One way to fight back against the enemy's lies is to change how you think and speak about what's going on. Replace the following statements with the more accurate statements:

"I feel..." (anger, fear, hate, worry, etc.)

Replace with:
"The enemy wants me to feel... But God says..."

"I think..." (there's no hope, God failed me, this won't work, no one loves me, etc.)

Replace with:
"The enemy wants me to think... But God says..."

"I physically feel..." (sick, pain, disease, etc.)

Replace with:
"The enemy wants me to believe I have (this physical issue)... But God says..."

This is not a "once 'n' done" thought replacement. The enemy will try again and again to keep old thought patterns in place. Be prepared to repeat the replacement truth over and over and over again. Let the truth become a "mantra." This will help you separate yourself from the lies.

As you succeed in separating from the lie, it may get louder or more pronounced. The enemy wants you to feel you are losing, but in reality, you have the lie on the run. You're gaining ground! That's your queue to keep repeating truth and keep moving forward in this process.

Sample of Freedom Process
Week 27 Homework

Instructions
This is a sample of the process you will be going through for every category of lies we will address in the next three months. Please read it and get familiar with the concepts included. You may want to read it **out loud** since that will be what you will be doing for each prayer in each lesson for the rest of this unit. This process may feel repetitive or unnecessary, but there is power in our words. We bind and loose things in heaven and on earth with the spoken word. Choose to read every word out loud for every prayer the first time through each lesson. After that, when you're continuing to get rid of the same lies again as you continue to choose freedom, feel free to use your own words. There is no "magical power" in these specific words, but there is power in the concepts these words represent.

Prayer for Surrender
Father God, thank You for creating me, _____ (your name), in Your image. Thank You for designing me perfectly for Your calling on my life. As a loving Father, please show me who I am in You. Help me understand and separate the _____ (your name) You created from everything else. Help me see and understand how I've been influenced or controlled by anything other than Your Holy Spirit. I surrender my _____ (lie). Help me to identify and separate from any lies in this area that I'm still believing. Help me continue to see the _____ (your name) You created me to be without the _____ (lie). Amen.

Symptom Chart Exercise
Review the following table and consider which symptoms you've experienced. Mark all the symptoms that apply to you. Ask the Holy Spirit to guide you.

Later, if you are confused about what you are feeling or how the enemy is attacking you, this tool will become a resource to help you sift through the lies, so you can easily identify them and eliminate them.

Emotional Symptoms

Sample Symptom
Sample Symptom
Sample Symptom
Sample Symptom

Spiritual Symptoms

Sample Symptom
Sample Symptom
Sample Symptom
Sample Symptom

Sample Lie

Tangible Symptoms

Sample Symptom
Sample Symptom
Sample Symptom
Sample Symptom

Thought Symptoms

Sample Symptom
Sample Symptom
Sample Symptom
Sample Symptom

Processing Questions:

1. List the circumstances and relationships where _____ (lie) has played a role in your life. (For example: ... etc.)

2. How did _____ (lie) play a role in your childhood?

3. Where has _____ (lie) played a role in your relationships as an adult?

4. How has _____ (lie) affected your decisions?

5. How has _____ (lie) interfered with your relationship with God?

6. Are you ready to repent of _____ (lie) and let Jesus take it? _____

Instructions

Unforgiveness can actually block your ability to get rid of lies and receive healing. Write a list of people and situations you need to forgive. Next, use the prayer template to pray through all of the people/instances on your list. Pray them through as many times as necessary to have a clear conscience on forgiveness.

Prayer of Forgiveness

Father God, thank You for shining Your light into my life to expose any unforgiveness or bitterness still hiding. Because I want Your full forgiveness as bought for me through Jesus's death on the cross, I choose to forgive those who have hurt or offended me.

I forgive _____ for
_____.

I forgive You, God, for any perceived hurt or offense that I've held against you. Specifically,
_____.

As I fully accept God's forgiveness, I choose to forgive myself for _____.
I accept full forgiveness in Christ.

List:

People and situations I need to forgive:

_____

_____

_____

_____

_____

_____

_____

_____

_____

_____

_____

God: _____

_____

_____

_____

Myself: _____

_____

_____

_____

Instructions

First, make a list of specific lies you have believed surrounding the _____ (lie). Next, pray the Prayer of Repentance for each lie in your list *out loud*. Finally, pray the Prayer of Freedom for each lie in your list *out loud*.

List:

To identify the specific lies you will be repenting of and getting rid of, list the variations of _____ (lie) that you've inherited or practiced: *(For example:...)*

Prayer of Repentance

Father God, I come to You on behalf of myself and my generational heritage. I repent and disown all _____ (lie) that my forefathers or I have been in agreement with. I reject and turn away from _____ (lie), including _____ (specific examples) and ask for Your forgiveness as paid for by Jesus's blood on the cross of Calvary. I accept Your complete forgiveness that casts my sins away as far as the East is from the West.

Prayer for Freedom

In the name of Jesus Christ, by the power of the Holy Spirit, I bind _____ (lie). You will not be able to express yourself in any harmful way. I take authority over _____ (lie), including _____ (specific examples) and command you to leave me. I do not want you to be in my life in any shape or form. I command you to leave me and go to hell. I choose God's life and truth instead. Leave now and don't ever come back. You are not welcome here. Holy Spirit, please enforce this eviction. Thank you, Father God, for total and complete freedom from the lies of _____ (lie).

_____
_____
_____
_____
_____
_____
_____
_____
_____
_____
_____
_____
_____
_____
_____
_____
_____
_____
_____
_____
_____
_____
_____
_____
_____
_____
_____
_____
_____
_____
_____
_____
_____

Prayer for Healing

Father God, thank You so much for total and complete freedom from _____ (lie). Father, in Your loving mercy, I ask for You to heal any damage the enemy caused in my relationship with You, myself, or others due to _____ (lie). I ask that You restore and rebuild the healthy relationships You designed for me. Help me to connect to You in a deeper way. Please heal my spirit from any damage. Please bring peace and connection to my mind, will, and emotions. Rewire my soul to remove the old ruts of _____ (lie) and create new understanding and thought patterns aligned with Your truth.

Help me to celebrate myself as Your temple in a new way. Please connect my spirit, soul, and body to each other in the healthy ways You designed. Help me to reconnect and rebuild relationships with others as You guide me for my good and Your glory.

Father God, I ask for physical healing from any damage done by _____ (lie). I ask that You would heal and restore damage to my DNA, cellular structures, tissues, organs, and systems. Where creative miracles are needed, please recreate. Please heal the balance of hormones and chemicals in my body to reach homeostasis. Heal my body to work in the way You designed it to work without the interference of the enemy.

Thank You for complete healing, inside and out, head to toe, spirit, soul, and body! In Jesus's name, Amen.

ADDITIONAL HEALING NEEDED: Write below the specific healings you are asking God for today (diseases, difficult circumstances, etc.). Ask God for what you need.

> *Congratulations!! Awesome job praying through these prayers!! You'll want to pray through them again whenever you feel this lie is gaining ground in your life. Trauma triggers and old habits may reopen the door to these lies. Don't get discouraged. Just clear them out again. If you don't have your books handy, pray whatever God gives you to repent and get rid of the lies.*

Letter Exercise

Write a letter to your _____ (lie). Explain why you don't need to believe the lie any longer and write in detail the truth you are claiming and believing instead. Once it is complete, read the letter out loud. (Do not skip this step! There is power in words!)

Sample Plan to Fight Back
Week 27 Homework

As you move forward, the thoughts and emotions from _____ (lie) may tempt you to fall back into old patterns. It's important to have a plan to fight back so you're not caught off guard.

Review the list of strategies in the appendix. Which strategies will you use to stay free of _____ (lie)?

-
-
-
-
-
-

Next, use the _____ (lie) Symptom Chart found at the beginning of this homework to help create a plan to fight back.

1. Review the "Spiritual Symptoms" you marked for _____ (lie). In the "Prayers" section of the blank chart following, write a specific statement of faith or prayer for each symptom you marked.

2. Review the "Emotional Symptoms" you marked for _____ (lie). In the "Scriptures" section of the blank chart following, write specific scripture verses you will use as your "sword of spirit" for each emotional pattern you marked.

3. Review the "Thought Symptoms" you marked for _____ (lie). In the "God Says" section, write a specific statement beginning with "God says…" to replace each of the thought patterns you marked.

4. Review the "Tangible Symptoms" you marked for _____ (lie). In the "Action Steps" section, write the action steps you'll take to replace the tangible habits and behaviors you marked.

Scriptures

Action Steps

Plan To Fight
Sample

Prayers

God Says...

NOTES

Accountability Share

Make sure you share with a trusted person about your freedom from _____ (lie). Do not consider this lesson finished until you have shared. You'll be amazed at the transformative power it holds.

I will share the following:
- Answers to the processing questions
- My Plan to Fight Back
- New revelations or understanding about my past
- Feelings or thoughts I'm still struggling to replace
- Questions of confusion I may have about the lie or the process
- Feelings of shame or guilt that are still present

I will share them with _____ (name).

Cleaning House Exercise

List any items in your possession that represent _____ (lie).

-
-
-
-
-
-

Would you be willing to get rid of these items? What is God asking you to do?

Week 28

Cultural Influences

LISTENING GUIDE

In each culture throughout the world, the enemy has worked to institute practices that are against the Lord. This is part of his strategy to turn humanity against God. The enemy wants to draw us away from God so we are more susceptible to his lies. Lies align us with the enemy instead of God.

> *"...by your sorcery all the nations were deceived."*
>
> -Revelation 18:23 (NKJV)

Sinful cultural practices can seem obvious from the outside. For example, we in the US are quick to identify idol worship in India where it is culturally acceptable to worship many "gods" every day. We may identify Voodoo or Satanism as evil.

All "religious" practices that are not worshipping the One True God, Jesus Christ, and the Holy Spirit are sin. This includes Eastern meditation, new age practices, yoga, martial arts, mother earth, and all "other" religions.

NOTES

> *"Thou shalt have no other gods before me."*
>
> -Exodus 20:3 (KJV)

However, it is more difficult to identify how the enemy is drawing us away with "normal" socially acceptable practices in our own culture. The roots of many of these practices are harmful and open harmful spiritual doors.

> *"The idols speak deceitfully, diviners see visions that lie; they tell dreams that are false, they give comfort in vain. Therefore the people wander like sheep oppressed for lack of a shepherd."*
>
> -Zechariah 10:2 (NLT)

Do not to be deceived by lies simply because they are familiar and comfortable in the world. We must question everything and bring it to God. The excuse that "everyone is doing it" does not protect us from lies.

> *"Let no one be found among you who sacrifices their son or daughter in the fire, who practices divination or sorcery, interprets omens, engages in witchcraft, or casts spells, or who is a medium or spiritist or who consults the dead."*
>
> -Deuteronomy 18:10-11 (NIV)

Are we running to **anything** other than God to solve our problems?

Cultural practices that can interfere with our relationship with God:
- Martial arts of any type for protection
- Yoga, Pilates, Tai Chi, Eastern meditation for relaxation or peace
- Pharmakeia, medicine, naturopaths, white witchcraft, homeopathic meds, oils
- Eastern medicine, chiropractors for health
- Masonic, Moose, Shriners or other secret societies for connection, power, or influence
- Tarot cards, fortune telling
- Astrology for answers because of fear of the future
- Magnetic jewelry, lucky things, dreamcatchers, amulets, etc. for luck or protection
- Ouija boards, witchcraft, séances, idols, pagan religions, demonic movies for knowledge or power in the spirit world
- Religious spirits, religious control, cults, false prophecy, manipulation of God's children

NOTES

Keep an open mind. To be wise and not fall into the traps of the enemy, do not take any cultural practice for granted. Examine them all. Pray about whether you have trusted any of the cultural practices on the list as a replacement for trusting God. Research the roots of anything in the list above that you'd like to keep practicing. Ask God to show you His perspective.

The enemy may tell you that by participating in the cultural practices, you deserve to feel guilt and shame. Well take that shame OFF you! There's no judgment here!

We are not asking you to stop any of these practices out of performance, religious control, or fear. We are simply asking you to take these areas to God and ask for His revelation and conviction. Only stop or change those practices that the Holy Spirit convicts you of.

Trust that He will guide you closer to Him. But to receive that guidance, you must be surrendered with an openness to the possibility of conviction. Our goal, as always, is to come into greater alignment with God. We want to draw closer to Him to receive love and freedom from lies.

WEEKLY WORSHIP
"Slow Fade" by Casting Crowns

DISCUSSION QUESTIONS
1. Are you offended that any specific items are on the above list of cultural influences? If so, why?

2. If God asked you to stop participating with all of the items on the list and trust Him in that area (heath, protection, etc.), would you be willing? Which item on the list would be most difficult for you to release?

3. Do you find it difficult to believe God would (or could) intervene in your life if you trusted Him alone instead of these practices? Why?

Identifying Cultural Influences Worksheet
Week 28 Homework

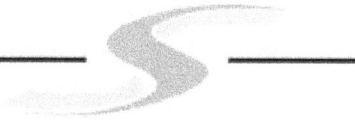

Instructions
We recommend you set aside a couple hours of uninterrupted time to work through the Freedom Process and Plan for Freedom. It's most helpful when you can do the entire homework in one sitting. If you need to pause to process or cry, we recommend doing so after the Prayer for Healing to reduce any opportunity for the enemy to distract. Get your tissues and chocolates ready. If it would be helpful for you, have worship music playing in the background. Remember, choose to read every word out loud for every prayer.

Prayer for Surrender
Father God, thank You for creating me, _____ (your name), in Your image. Thank You for designing me perfectly for Your calling on my life. As a loving Father, please show me who I am in You. Help me understand and separate the _____ (your name) You created from everything else. Help me see and understand how I've been influenced or controlled by anything other than Your Holy Spirit. I surrender my **cultural influences**. Help me to identify and separate from any lies in this area that I'm still believing. Help me continue to see the _____ (your name) You created me to be without the **cultural influences**. Amen.

Symptom Chart Exercise
Review the following table and consider which symptoms you've experienced. Mark all the symptoms that apply to you. Ask the Holy Spirit to guide you.

Later, if you are confused about what you are feeling or how the enemy is attacking you, this tool will become a resource to help you sift through the lies, so you can easily identify them and eliminate them.

Emotional Symptoms

Persistent fear of change or loss
Persistent fear that God will not help
Feelings of being alone
Feeling uncared for
Feeling forgotten
Feeling unsafe
Catastrophizing
Dread
Tormenting emotional spirals

Tangible Symptoms

Exhaustion and weariness
Sleeplessness or insomnia
Disorientation, vertigo, dizziness
Nightmares, night terrors, or bad dreams
Problems with vision
Physical reliance on practice, placebo effect
Disease or illness related to anxiety
Disease or illness related to the cultural practice
Addiction to the practice of influence
Participating in other religious practices
Joining cults or secret societies
Practicing magic

Cultural Influences

Spiritual Symptoms

Separation from God
Disbelief in God's ability to participate in our life
Disbelief in God's desire to participate in our life
Lack of peace
Difficulty reading or understanding Scripture
Difficulty praying
Difficulty worshipping

Thought Symptoms

Cyclical thoughts, consistent nagging thoughts
Rationalizing that there are immediate benefits in one area
Rationalizing that it cannot hurt you because you don't
    understand how it could be damaging.
Downplaying the power of the enemy.
Believing that you need this thing/practice
Confusion or disorientation
"But I know Christians who do that."
"But I need this for my health/protection/peace of mind"
"But they do it and they look prosperous."
"This practice is healthy for my body, so it can't be
    unhealthy for my soul or spirit."

Processing Questions:

1. List the circumstances and relationships where **cultural influences** have played a role in your life. *(For example: yoga, tarot cards, Ouija boards, fortune telling, naturopathic medicine, martial arts, other religions, entertainment about witchcraft, fantasy, horror, etc.)*

2. How did **cultural influences** play a role in your childhood?

3. Where have **cultural influences** played a role in your relationships as an adult?

4. How have **cultural influences** affected your decisions?

5. How have **cultural influences** interfered with your relationship with God?

6. Are you ready to repent of **cultural influences** and let Jesus take it? _____

Instructions

Unforgiveness can actually block your ability to get rid of lies and receive healing. Write a list of people and situations you need to forgive. Next, use the prayer template to pray through all of the people/instances on your list. Pray them through as many times as necessary to have a clear conscience on forgiveness.

Prayer of Forgiveness

Father God, thank You for shining Your light into my life to expose any unforgiveness or bitterness still hiding. Because I want Your full forgiveness as bought for me through Jesus's death on the cross, I choose to forgive those who have hurt or offended me.

I forgive _____ for
_____.

I forgive You, God, for any perceived hurt or offense that I've held against you. Specifically, _____.

As I fully accept God's forgiveness, I choose to forgive myself for _____.
I accept full forgiveness in Christ.

List:

People and situations I need to forgive:

_____

_____

_____

_____

_____

_____

_____

_____

_____

_____

_____

God: _____

_____

_____

_____

Myself: _____

_____

_____

_____

Instructions
First, make a list of specific lies you have believed surrounding the **cultural influences.** Next, pray the Prayer of Repentance for each lie in your list *out loud*. Finally, pray the Prayer of Freedom for each lie in your list *out loud*.

List:
To identify the specific lies you will be repenting of and getting rid of, list the variations of **cultural influences** that you've inherited or practiced: *(For example: yoga, tarot cards, Ouija boards, fortune telling, naturopathic medicine, martial arts, other religions, entertainment about witchcraft, fantasy, horror, etc.)*

Prayer of Repentance
Father God, I come to You on behalf of myself and my generational heritage. I repent and disown all **cultural influences** that my forefathers or I have been in agreement with. I reject and turn away from **cultural influences**, including _____ (specific examples) and ask for Your forgiveness as paid for by Jesus's blood on the cross of Calvary. I accept Your complete forgiveness that casts my sins away as far as the East is from the West.

Prayer for Freedom
In the name of Jesus Christ, by the power of the Holy Spirit, I bind **cultural influences**. You will not be able to express yourself in any harmful way. I take authority over **cultural influences**, including _____ (specific examples) and command you to leave me. I do not want you to be in my life in any shape or form. I command you to leave me and go to hell. I choose God's life and truth instead. Leave now and don't ever come back. You are not welcome here. Holy Spirit, please enforce this eviction. Thank you, Father God, for total and complete freedom from the lies of **cultural influences**.

_____
_____
_____
_____
_____
_____
_____
_____
_____
_____
_____
_____
_____
_____
_____
_____
_____
_____
_____
_____
_____
_____
_____
_____
_____
_____
_____
_____
_____
_____
_____

Prayer for Healing

Father God, thank You so much for total and complete freedom from **cultural influences**. Father, in Your loving mercy, I ask for You to heal any damage the enemy caused in my relationship with You, myself, or others due to **cultural influences**. I ask that You restore and rebuild the healthy relationships You designed for me. Help me to connect to You in a deeper way. Please heal my spirit from any damage. Please bring peace and connection to my mind, will, and emotions. Rewire my soul to remove the old ruts of **cultural influences** and create new understanding and thought patterns aligned with Your truth.

Help me to celebrate myself as Your temple in a new way. Please connect my spirit, soul, and body to each other in the healthy ways You designed. Help me to reconnect and rebuild relationships with others as You guide me for my good and Your glory.

Father God, I ask for physical healing from any damage done by **cultural influences**. I ask that You would heal and restore damage to my DNA, cellular structures, tissues, organs, and systems. Where creative miracles are needed, please recreate. Please heal the balance of hormones and chemicals in my body to reach homeostasis. Heal my body to work in the way You designed it to work without the interference of the enemy.

Thank You for complete healing, inside and out, head to toe, spirit, soul, and body! In Jesus's name, Amen.

ADDITIONAL HEALING NEEDED: Write below the specific healings you are asking God for today (diseases, difficult circumstances, etc.). Ask God for what you need.

Congratulations!! Awesome job praying through these prayers!! You'll want to pray through them again whenever you feel this lie is gaining ground in your life. Trauma triggers and old habits may reopen the door to these lies. Don't get discouraged. Just clear them out again. If you don't have your books handy, pray whatever God gives you to repent and get rid of the lies.

Letter Exercise

Write a letter to your **cultural influences**. Explain why you don't need to believe the lie any longer and write in detail the truth you are claiming and believing instead. Once it is complete, read the letter out loud. (Do not skip this step! There is power in words!)

Plan to Fight Back
Week 28 Homework

As you move forward, the thoughts and emotions from **cultural influences** may tempt you to fall back into old patterns. It's important to have a plan to fight back so you're not caught off guard.

Review the list of strategies in the appendix. Which strategies will you use to stay free of **cultural influences**?

-
-
-
-
-
-

Next, use the **Cultural Influences** Symptom Chart found at the beginning of this homework to help create a plan to fight back.

1. Review the "Spiritual Symptoms" you marked for **cultural influences**. In the "Prayers" section of the blank chart following, write a specific statement of faith or prayer for each symptom you marked.

2. Review the "Emotional Symptoms" you marked for **cultural influences**. In the "Scriptures" section of the blank chart following, write specific scripture verses you will use as your "sword of spirit" for each emotional pattern you marked.

3. Review the "Thought Symptoms" you marked for **cultural influences**. In the "God Says" section, write a specific statement beginning with "God says…" to replace each of the thought patterns you marked.

4. Review the "Tangible Symptoms" you marked for **cultural influences**. In the "Action Steps" section, write the action steps you'll take to replace the tangible habits and behaviors you marked.

Scriptures

Action Steps

Cultural Influences

Prayers

God Says...

NOTES

Accountability Share

Make sure you share with a trusted person about your freedom from **cultural influences**. Do not consider this lesson finished until you have shared. You'll be amazed at the transformative power it holds.

I will share the following:
- Answers to the processing questions
- My plan to fight back
- New revelations or understanding about my past
- Feelings or thoughts I'm still struggling to replace
- Questions of confusion I may have about the lie or the process
- Feelings of shame or guilt that are still present

I will share them with _____ (name).

Exercise: Getting Rid of Cultural Influence Items

Now that we've gotten rid of the lies attached to cultural influences, it's time to clean house. We don't want to give the enemy any room in our lives to come back in. Now is the time to ask the Holy Spirit to help us identify and physically get rid of all symbols or items related to those lies.

List any items in your possession that represent **cultural influences**.

-
-
-
-
-
-

Would you be willing to get rid of these items? What is God asking you to do?

Ask God to show you any cultural influence items in these categories that need to be removed from your life:

- Books
- Movies, DVD's
- Educational materials
- Music, CD's
- Board games, cards, digital games
- Jewelry, crystals, magnetics
- Decorations, art, statues, trinkets, souvenirs
- Clothes
- Furniture
- Exercise related items – yoga, martial arts, etc.
- Medicine related – homeopathic, vitamin, oil or other

REMOVE ITEMS ASAP!

Week 29

Passing the Buck

LISTENING GUIDE

It's no secret that life is easier without responsibilities. Many of us have centered our lives around "living for the weekend." Vacation becomes the reason we can get through three more weeks of work.

There's no doubt our quality of life improves with regular time to rest and recharge. On the other hand, there are spiritual, emotional, and physical consequences when we refuse to take responsibility.

Do you try to avoid the difficult conversations? Or avoid taking ownership of your flaws? Or avoid stepping into opportunities God has opened for you because they are "too hard?" Have you gotten really good at making excuses for staying home or backing out?

Owning Responsibilities:
God is responsible for a lot—creating the universe, designing His children, reconciling us to Himself, orchestrating our provision, and working all things for our good (just to name a few). Could you imagine if one day God believed a lie and decided not to be responsible for those things anymore?

God doesn't ask us to be completely responsible for our lives, but He does want us to take an active part in His Kingdom while we are here. God has a plan for us to heal and grow. We are required to actively participate in His plan.

NOTES

Enjoying the feelings of having a loving God is not enough to experience life to the full. If we don't take responsibility and aren't obedient to God, then we are turning away from God. Separation from God has consequences.

Passiveness is refusing to take ownership or blame shifting.

Symptoms of Passiveness:
- Believing your contribution isn't necessary because someone else will take care of God's Kingdom, your family or community, the church, etc.
- Refusal to make decisions so you can blame others
- Thinking "If only they would…"
- Asking "What's the point of taking action?"
- Denying personal responsibility
- Avoidance
- Mixed messages
- Procrastination or stalling
- Forgetting
- Not making necessary decisions

Owning Faults:
The blame game started way back in the Garden of Eden. Adam said, "Eve made me do it!" Then Eve said, "The serpent made me do it!"

Many times, we shirk ownership of our sins or faults out of fear of punishment, fear of consequences, or living with shame. But hiding our flaws is what keeps us stuck in our shame. It allows the lies we believe to continue to take up residence in our lives.

> *"But everything exposed by the light becomes visible--and everything that is illuminated becomes a light."*
>
> -Ephesians 5:13 (NIV)

God's heart is for us to be free of the lies that torment us. We must be willing to own our faults and share them with a trusted sponsor or mentor. God will guide us to the right person in the right time if we ask Him for help and courage.

> *"Therefore confess your sins to each other and pray for each other so that you may be healed. The prayer of a righteous person is powerful and effective."*
>
> -James 5:16 (NIV)

NOTES

Often, we are not consciously aware that we are shifting our responsibilities and faults onto another person. We truly believe that others are to blame. And while others may shoulder some responsibility, we usually have a portion that we are not admitting.

For example, we may be responsible for failing to exercise forgiveness, standing up for ourselves, creating healthy boundaries, addressing confrontation, or asking for what we need. Once we can recognize our shortcomings, we more easily forgive both others and ourselves.

Life is complex and rarely black and white. Trying to fit blame and responsibility entirely onto someone else can be exhausting and keep us in denial of the truth. Accepting shades of gray and owning some responsibility may not be comfortable at first, but it will bring peace to our souls.

Important Note:
Victims who have been hurt by abusers should never take on responsibility for the abuse. The abuser is the one who ultimately decided to carry out the abuse. That is not blame shifting. That is simply putting the responsibility where it belongs.

A false sense of responsibility can be just as damaging as passiveness. We will address a false sense of responsibility in more detail in a later chapter.

By trying to avoid responsibility, we can fall into a pattern of unhealthy behavior called Passive Aggression. This is anger expressed in a passive manner. It often works hand in hand with the lies of victim mentality.

Symptoms of Passive Aggression:
- Stonewalling
- Withholding resources or information
- Professional exclusion
- Excuse making
- Blaming
- Breaking agreements
- Lack of follow through
- Resistance
- Stubbornness
- Rigidity
- Inefficiency, complication, incompletion, or ruination of tasks
- Backstabbing
- Two-faced
- Mixed messages
- Expecting others to pick up on unspoken queues

NOTES

Passive aggression is generally a poor coping tool we use to deflect our fear or insecurities. We don't have to stay stuck in this destructive pattern, though. We can combat these behaviors by:

- Recognizing that our anger is masking our fears
- Getting honest with ourselves about our insecurities and fears
- Discussing these fears with someone we trust
- Releasing the emotions in more productive ways like exercise or tears
- Creating healthy boundaries that will keep us safe and balanced
- Forgiving those who have hurt us
- Addressing our feelings with those who have hurt us in a calm, rational conversation when possible

WEEKLY WORSHIP
"Starts with Me" by Tim Timmons

DISCUSSION QUESTIONS

1. Have you ever considered passiveness to be an issue for you? If not, has this lesson changed your perspective?

2. Which symptoms of passive aggression in the list above can you identify with?

3. How can you use Strategy #1 - Get Honest with Yourself to counteract some of the passiveness you are being tempted by?

NOTES

Passing the Buck Worksheet
Week 29 Homework

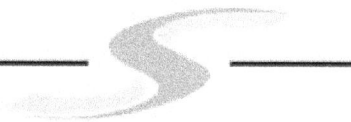

Instructions
We recommend you set aside a couple hours of uninterrupted time to work through the Freedom Process and Plan for Freedom. It's most helpful when you can do the entire homework in one sitting. If you need to pause to process or cry, we recommend doing so after the Prayer for Healing to reduce any opportunity for the enemy to distract. Get your tissues and chocolates ready. If it would be helpful for you, have worship music playing in the background. Remember, choose to read every word out loud for every prayer.

Prayer for Surrender
Father God, thank You for creating me, _____ (your name), in Your image. Thank You for designing me perfectly for Your calling on my life. As a loving Father, please show me who I am in You. Help me understand and separate the _____ (your name) You created from everything else. Help me see and understand how I've been influenced or controlled by anything other than Your Holy Spirit. I surrender my **passiveness and passive aggressiveness**. Help me to identify and separate from any lies in this area that I'm still believing. Help me continue to see the _____ (your name) You created me to be without the **passiveness and passive aggressiveness**.

Symptom Chart Exercise
Review the following table and consider which symptoms you've experienced. Mark all the symptoms that apply to you. Ask the Holy Spirit to guide you.

Later, if you are confused about what you are feeling or how the enemy is attacking you, this tool will become a resource to help you sift through the lies, so you can easily identify them and eliminate them.

Emotional Symptoms

Fear of responsibility
Fear of confrontation
Feeling unheard
Feeling invisible
Resentment
Depression
Hopelessness/Powerlessness
Suppressed anger
Secret desire for revenge

Tangible Symptoms

Abdicating responsibility
Deflecting or deferring
Lack of accountability
Avoiding others or trying to blend in
Withholding connection from others
Staying silent or refusing to communicate
  with words
Exhaustion
Tardiness
Saying "Sure/Fine/Whatever"
Saying "I'm OK" when I'm not OK
Selective forgetting or feigning forgetting

Passiveness & Passive-Aggressiveness

Spiritual Symptoms

God will take care of everything for me without my participation
I'm a good person and that's enough for God.
I don't have to own my mistakes because I had good intentions
God will just forgive my sins, I don't have to actively avoid them
God doesn't need me to serve
God can't use me anyway
I'm not good enough to help God
I'll keep people happy instead of standing up for God's truth

Thought Symptoms

Avoiding thoughts of problems and problem solving
Forgetfulness
Ruminating on resentment and fantasizing revenge
"That's someone else's job/responsibility."
"I don't have a voice or a say."
"I cannot risk sharing my views."
"I am too scared to share my thoughts."
"I don't want to be a bother."
"I'm too scared to say no."
"I don't want to be at fault."
"I don't want to be responsible. I'll only fail."
"I think it's wrong, but I don't want to rock the boat."
"I'll show them..."

Passiveness Questions:

1. List the circumstances and relationships where **passiveness** has played a role in your life.
   (For example: abdicating responsibilities, refusal to decide, lack of stepping up or volunteering, etc.)

2. How did **passiveness** play a role in your childhood?

3. Where has **passiveness** played a role in your relationships as an adult?

4. How has **passiveness** affected your decisions?

5. How has **passiveness** interfered with your relationship with God?

6. Are you ready to repent of **passiveness** and let Jesus take it? _____

Passive Aggressiveness Questions:
1. List the circumstances and relationships where **passive aggressiveness** has played a role in your life. *(For example: excuse making, blaming, broken agreements, lack of follow through, tardiness, etc.)*

2. How did **passive aggressiveness** play a role in your childhood?

3. Where has **passive aggressiveness** played a role in your relationships as an adult?

4. How has **passive aggressiveness** affected your decisions?

5. How has **passive aggressiveness** interfered with your relationship with God?

6. Are you ready to repent for **passive aggressiveness** and let Jesus take it? _____

Instructions

Unforgiveness can actually block your ability to get rid of lies and receive healing. Write a list of people and situations you need to forgive. Next, use the prayer template to pray through all of the people/instances on your list. Pray them through as many times as necessary to have a clear conscience on forgiveness.

Prayer of Forgiveness

Father God, thank You for shining Your light into my life to expose any unforgiveness or bitterness still hiding. Because I want Your full forgiveness as bought for me through Jesus's death on the cross, I choose to forgive those who have hurt or offended me.

I forgive _____ for

_____.

I forgive You, God, for any perceived hurt or offense that I've held against you. Specifically,

_____.

As I fully accept God's forgiveness, I choose to forgive myself for _____.
I accept full forgiveness in Christ.

List:

People and situations I need to forgive:

_____

_____

_____

_____

_____

_____

_____

_____

_____

_____

_____

God: _____

_____

_____

_____

Myself: _____

_____

_____

_____

Instructions

First, make a list of specific lies you have believed surrounding the **passiveness and passive aggressiveness**. Next, pray the Prayer of Repentance for each lie in your list *out loud*. Finally, pray the Prayer of Freedom for each lie in your list *out loud*.

List

To identify the specific lies you will be repenting of and getting rid of, list the variations of **passiveness and passive aggressiveness** that you've inherited or practiced: *(For example: abdicating responsibilities, refusal to decide, lack of stepping up or volunteering, excuse making, blaming, broken agreements, lack of follow through, tardiness, etc.)*

Prayer of Repentance

Father God, I come to You on behalf of myself and my generational heritage. I repent and disown all **passiveness and passive aggressiveness** that my forefathers or I have been in agreement with. I reject and turn away from **passiveness and passive aggressiveness**, including _____ (specific examples) and ask for Your forgiveness as paid for by Jesus's blood on the cross of Calvary. I accept Your complete forgiveness that casts my sins away as far as the East is from the West.

Prayer for Freedom

In the name of Jesus Christ, by the power of the Holy Spirit, I bind **passiveness and passive aggressiveness**. You will not be able to express yourself in any harmful way. I take authority over **passiveness and passive aggressiveness**, including _____ (specific examples) and command you to leave me. I do not want you to be in my life in any shape or form. I command you to leave me and go to hell. I choose God's life and truth instead. Leave now and don't ever come back. You are not welcome here. Holy Spirit, please enforce this eviction. Thank you, Father God, for total and complete freedom from the lies of **passiveness and passive aggressiveness**.

Prayer for Healing

Father God, thank You so much for total and complete freedom from **passiveness and passive aggressiveness**. Father, in Your loving mercy, I ask for You to heal any damage the enemy caused in my relationship with You, myself, or others due to **passiveness and passive aggressiveness**. I ask that You restore and rebuild the healthy relationships You designed for me. Help me to connect to You in a deeper way. Please heal my spirit from any damage. Please bring peace and connection to my mind, will, and emotions. Rewire my soul to remove the old ruts of **passiveness and passive aggressiveness** and create new understanding and thought patterns aligned with Your truth. Help me to celebrate myself as Your temple in a new way. Please connect my spirit, soul, and body to each other in the healthy ways You designed. Help me to reconnect and rebuild relationships with others as You guide me for my good and Your glory.

Father God, I ask for physical healing from any damage done by **passiveness and passive aggressiveness**. I ask that You would heal and restore damage to my DNA, cellular structures, tissues, organs, and systems. Where creative miracles are needed, please recreate. Please heal the balance of hormones and chemicals in my body to reach homeostasis. Heal my body to work in the way You designed it to work without the interference of the enemy.

Thank You for complete healing, inside and out, head to toe, spirit, soul, and body! In Jesus's name, Amen.

ADDITIONAL HEALING NEEDED: Write below the specific healings you are asking God for today (diseases, difficult circumstances, etc.). Ask God for what you need.

Congratulations!! Awesome job praying through these prayers!! You'll want to pray through them again whenever you feel this lie is gaining ground in your life. Trauma triggers and old habits may reopen the door to these lies. Don't get discouraged. Just clear them out again. If you don't have your books handy, pray whatever God gives you to repent and get rid of the lies.

Letter Exercise

Write a letter to your **passiveness and passive aggressiveness**. Explain why you don't need to believe the lie any longer and write in detail the truth you are claiming and believing instead. Once it is complete, read the letter out loud. (Do not skip this step! There is power in words!)

Plan to Fight Back
Week 29 Homework

As you move forward, the thoughts and emotions from **passiveness and passive aggressiveness** may tempt you to fall back into old patterns. It's important to have a plan to fight back so you're not caught off guard.

Review the list of strategies in the appendix. Which strategies will you use to stay free of **passiveness and passive aggressiveness**?

-
-
-
-
-
-

Next, use the **Passiveness and Passive Aggressiveness** Symptoms Chart found at the beginning of this homework to help create a plan to fight back.

1. Review the "Spiritual Symptoms" you marked for **passiveness and passive aggressiveness**. In the "Prayers" section of the blank chart following, write a specific statement of faith or prayer for each symptom you marked.

2. Review the "Emotional Symptoms" you marked for **passiveness and passive aggressiveness.** In the "Scriptures" section of the blank chart following, write specific scripture verses you will use as your "sword of spirit" for each emotional pattern you marked.

3. Review the "Thought Symptoms" you marked for **passiveness and passive aggressiveness**. In the "God Says" section, write a specific statement beginning with "God says…" to replace each of the thought patterns you marked.

4. Review the "Tangible Symptoms" you marked for **passiveness and passive aggressiveness**. In the "Action Steps" section, write the action steps you'll take to replace the tangible habits and behaviors you marked.

Scriptures

Action Steps

Passiveness & Passive-
Aggressiveness

Prayers

God Says...

Accountability Share

Make sure you share with a trusted person about your freedom from **passiveness and passive aggressiveness**. Do not consider this lesson finished until you have shared. You'll be amazed at the transformative power it holds.

I will share the following:
- Answers to the processing questions
- My plan to fight back
- New revelations or understanding about my past
- Feelings or thoughts I'm still struggling to replace
- Questions of confusion I may have about the lie or the process
- Feelings of shame or guilt that are still present

I will share them with _____ (name).

Cleaning House Exercise

List any items in your possession that represent **passiveness and passive aggressiveness**.

-
-
-
-
-
-

Would you be willing to get rid of these items? What is God asking you to do?

Denial and Lying Worksheet
Week 29 Homework

Instructions

We recommend you set aside a couple hours of uninterrupted time to work through the Freedom Process and Plan for Freedom. It's most helpful when you can do the entire homework in one sitting. If you need to pause to process or cry, we recommend doing so after the Prayer for Healing to reduce any opportunity for the enemy to distract. Get your tissues and chocolates ready. If it would be helpful for you, have worship music playing in the background. Remember, choose to read every word out loud for every prayer.

Prayer for Surrender

Father God, thank You for creating me, _____ (your name), in Your image. Thank You for designing me perfectly for Your calling on my life. As a loving Father, please show me who I am in You. Help me understand and separate the _____ (your name) You created from everything else. Help me see and understand how I've been influenced or controlled by anything other than Your Holy Spirit. I surrender my **denial and lying**. Help me to identify and separate from any lies in this area that I'm still believing. Help me continue to see the _____ (your name) You created me to be without the **denial and lying**.

Symptom Chart Exercise

Review the following table and consider which symptoms you've experienced. Mark all the symptoms that apply to you. Ask the Holy Spirit to guide you.

Later, if you are confused about what you are feeling or how the enemy is attacking you, this tool will become a resource to help you sift through the lies, so you can easily identify them and eliminate them.

Emotional Symptoms

Defensiveness
Flashes of anger
Lack of empathy
Disconnected from emotions
Intense emotions that do not fit the situation
Fear of being found out
Fear of losing position, power, or influence

Tangible Symptoms

Avoidance of people, places, or things
Headaches
Digestive Issues
Numbness
Chemical Addictions
Alzheimer's or Dementia

Denial & Lying

Spiritual Symptoms

Separation from God
Distrust of God, self, or others
Fantasy; lack of reality
Distorted understanding of the Bible
Disconnected from Truth
Lack of conviction related to sin
Hardened conscience
Difficulty hearing the Holy Spirit

Thought Symptoms

Categorically refusing to look at a topic or memory
Justifying avoidance or lying as self-preservation
Strategizing possible outcomes if truth is found out
Attempting to position or control others' opinions
Using absolutes in defense to self or others
Accusing others to move the spotlight elsewhere
Downplaying significance of events, lies, white-lies, or omissions
"There's no way! You're crazy!"
"They are the ones who…"
"It's not a big deal…"
"Let it stay in the past."
"It's safer not to feel."
"The truth could impact my life too much."

Processing Questions:

1. List the circumstances and relationships where **denial and lying** have played a role in your life. *(For example: "I don't want to think about that," selective forgetting, "I never did that," blaming others, etc.)*

2. How did **denial and lying** play a role in your childhood?

3. Where have **denial and lying** played a role in your relationships as an adult?

4. How have **denial and lying** affected your decisions?

5. How have **denial and lying** interfered with your relationship with God?

6. Are you ready to repent of **denial and lying** and let Jesus take them? _____

Instructions

Unforgiveness can actually block your ability to get rid of lies and receive healing. Write a list of people and situations you need to forgive. Next, use the prayer template to pray through all of the people/instances on your list. Pray them through as many times as necessary to have a clear conscience on forgiveness.

Prayer of Forgiveness

Father God, thank You for shining Your light into my life to expose any unforgiveness or bitterness still hiding. Because I want Your full forgiveness as bought for me through Jesus's death on the cross, I choose to forgive those who have hurt or offended me.

I forgive _____ for
_____.

I forgive You, God, for any perceived hurt or offense that I've held against you. Specifically, _____.

As I fully accept God's forgiveness, I choose to forgive myself for _____.
I accept full forgiveness in Christ.

List:

People and situations I need to forgive:

_____
_____
_____
_____
_____
_____
_____
_____
_____
_____
_____

God: _____
_____
_____
_____

Myself: _____
_____
_____
_____

Instructions

First, make a list of specific lies you have believed surrounding the **denial and lying**. Next, pray the Prayer of Repentance for each lie in your list *out loud*. Finally, pray the Prayer of Freedom for each lie in your list *out loud*.

List

To identify the specific lies you will be repenting of and getting rid of, list the variations of **denial and lying** that you've inherited or practiced: *(For example: "I don't want to think about that," selective forgetting, "I never did that," blaming others, etc.)*

Prayer of Repentance

Father God, I come to You on behalf of myself and my generational heritage. I repent and disown all **denial and lying** that my forefathers or I have been in agreement with. I reject and turn away from **denial and lying**, including _____ (specific examples) and ask for Your forgiveness as paid for by Jesus's blood on the cross of Calvary. I accept Your complete forgiveness that casts my sins away as far as the East is from the West.

Prayer for Freedom

In the name of Jesus Christ, by the power of the Holy Spirit, I bind **denial and lying**. You will not be able to express yourself in any harmful way. I take authority over **denial and lying**, including _____ (specific examples) and command you to leave me. I do not want you to be in my life in any shape or form. I command you to leave me and go to hell. I choose God's life and truth instead. Leave now and don't ever come back. You are not welcome here. Holy Spirit, please enforce this eviction. Thank you, Father God, for total and complete freedom from the lies of **denial and lying**.

_____
_____
_____
_____
_____
_____
_____
_____
_____
_____
_____
_____
_____
_____
_____
_____
_____
_____
_____
_____
_____
_____
_____
_____
_____
_____

Prayer for Healing

Father God, thank You so much for total and complete freedom from **denial and lying**. Father, in Your loving mercy, I ask for You to heal any damage the enemy caused in my relationship with You, myself or others due to **denial and lying**. I ask that You restore and rebuild the healthy relationships You designed for me. Help me to connect to You in a deeper way. Please heal my spirit from any damage. Please bring peace and connection to my mind, will, and emotions. Rewire my soul to remove the old ruts of **denial and lying** and create new understanding and thought patterns aligned with Your truth. Help me to celebrate myself as Your temple in a new way. Please connect my spirit, soul, and body to each other in the healthy ways You designed. Help me to reconnect and rebuild relationships with others as You guide me for my good and Your glory.

Father God, I ask for physical healing from any damage done by **denial and lying**. I ask that You would heal and restore damage to my DNA, cellular structures, tissues, organs, and systems. Where creative miracles are needed, please recreate. Please heal the balance of hormones and chemicals in my body to reach homeostasis. Heal my body to work in the way You designed it to work without the interference of the enemy.

Thank You for complete healing, inside and out, head to toe, spirit, soul, and body! In Jesus's name, Amen.

ADDITIONAL HEALING NEEDED: Write below the specific healings you are asking God for today (diseases, difficult circumstances, etc.). Ask God for what you need.

Congratulations!! Awesome job praying through these prayers!! You'll want to pray through them again whenever you feel this lie is gaining ground in your life. Trauma triggers and old habits may reopen the door to these lies. Don't get discouraged. Just clear them out again. If you don't have your books handy, pray whatever God gives you to repent and get rid of the lies.

Letter Exercise

Write a letter to your **denial and lying**. Explain why you don't need to believe the lies any longer and write in detail the truth you are claiming and believing instead. Once it is complete, read the letter out loud. (Do not skip this step! There is power in words!)

Plan to Fight Back
Week 29 Homework

As you move forward, the thoughts and emotions from **denial and lying** may tempt you to fall back into old patterns. It's important to have a plan to fight back so you're not caught off guard.

Review the list of strategies in the appendix. Which strategies will you use to stay free of **denial and lying**?

-
-
-
-
-
-

Next, use the **denial and lying** Symptom Chart found at the beginning of this homework to help create a plan to fight back.

1. Review the "Spiritual Symptoms" you marked for **denial and lying**. In the "Prayers" section of the blank chart following, write a specific statement of faith or prayer for each symptom you marked.

2. Review the "Emotional Symptoms" you marked for **denial and lying**. In the "Scriptures" section of the blank chart following, write specific scripture verses you will use as your "sword of spirit" for each emotional pattern you marked.

3. Review the "Thought Symptoms" you marked for **denial and lying**. In the "God Says" section, write a specific statement beginning with "God says…" to replace each of the thought patterns you marked.

4. Review the "Tangible Symptoms" you marked for **denial and lying**. In the "Action Steps" section, write the action steps you'll take to replace the tangible habits and behaviors you marked.

Scriptures

Action Steps

Denial & Lying

Prayers

God Says...

NOTES

Accountability Share

Make sure you share with a trusted person about your freedom from **denial and lying**. Do not consider this lesson finished until you have shared. You'll be amazed at the transformative power it holds.

I will share the following:
- Answers to the processing questions
- My plan to fight back
- New revelations or understanding about my past
- Feelings or thoughts I'm still struggling to replace
- Questions of confusion I may have about the lie or the process
- Feelings of shame or guilt that are still present

I will share them with _____ (name).

Cleaning House Exercise

List any items in your possession that represent **denial and lying**.

-
-
-
-
-
-

Would you be willing to get rid of these items? What is God asking you to do?

Week 30

Victim Mentality

LISTENING GUIDE

A mentality is a perspective that frames the way we see ourselves, our story, and those around us. Therefore, the victim mentality is a lie that can shade (or warp) our perspective of every circumstance or interaction. **Victim mentality can actually be woven into our version of reality without our awareness.**

This week we'll take a step back and open ourselves to the possibility of seeing our story from a different perspective. We'll need to get honest with ourselves and question how we interpret both the wonderful and painful events in our lives.

Example:
You go to a coffee shop after work to meet a friend, but when you arrive, you get a message that they will have to work late and are no longer able to meet you. What is your first reaction?

When we agree with **victim mentality**, our first reaction will be to assume this was done deliberately. We will perceive this circumstance as our lot in life to be the one who's dismissed. We could perceive it's our color, gender, personality, height, weight, religion, appearance, etc. that got us dismissed. Or, we could think it's the "perpetrator's" position, gender, color, status, religion, appearance, etc. that made them dismiss us.

When we agree with **self-pity**, we might think about how we've gone out of our way for nothing or feel as if we are not valued by our friend. We may even forget all about the ten other times this friend kept their promise to meet. We may get sucked into a "poor me" spiral.

NOTES

Symptoms of Victim Mentality:
- Believing you deserve to get hurt or abused
- Being the "whipping boy" for those around you
- Believing you deserve less than others
- Feeling powerless to change your circumstances
- Adopting cynical and/or pessimistic attitudes
- Believing others are purposely trying to hurt you
- Seeing small hurdles as much larger catastrophes
- Feeling attacked when you're given constructive criticism
- Regularly putting yourself down
- Having a poverty mindset
- Living with a "chip on the shoulder"
- Believing others are "always" prejudiced against you because of color, gender, weight, education, ethnicity, etc.

Symptoms of Self-Pity:
- Thinking "poor me, my life is worse"
- Blaming other people or situations for your negative feelings
- Voluntarily wallowing in past painful memories where you felt like a victim
- Focusing on complaints, even when things go right
- Feeling attacked when you're given constructive criticism
- Refusing to consider other perspectives when it comes to problems
- Feeling unable to cope effectively with a problem or life in general
- Taking enjoyment or comfort in feeling sorry for yourself and sharing your tragic stories
- Believing everyone else is better off or has an easier life than you
- Expecting to receive sympathy and feeling cheated if you do not receive it
- Attempting to "one-up" others by sharing troubles or traumatic experiences

The lie of self-pity tells us that we and our problems are at the center of the story. Problems are not simply happening, they are happening *to us* frequently, unjustly, and without hope to change our situation.

However, we are not powerless to change our perspective and our actions. We cannot change others, but we can change ourselves.

Consider the example of the canceled meeting from a different perspective. A healthy mentality could have compassion on the friend working late, be confident that God is working all things for good, and assume that God may have different, unexpected blessings instead.

To come out of **victim mentality** and **self-pity**, start using these strategies:

Taking Thoughts Captive (Strategy #17)
- Practice being mindful about your thoughts and where they lead.
- Recognize when you are focusing on your struggles.
- Actively redirect your thoughts when wallowing in pain or cynicism.

NOTES

Keeping an **Eternal Perspective** (Strategy #25)
- Try to see your circumstances as a larger part of God's plan.
- Recognize that God's plan for each person is different and cannot be compared.
- Stay aware that your enemy is not made of flesh and blood.
- Expect to be tempted in your mind and emotions.

Understanding Your Intrinsic Value (Strategy #8)
- Remember that you are loved and valuable to God despite circumstances.
- No matter how you are treated by people, God loves you.
- You can be forgiven by God no matter how many times you mess up.

Setting **Healthy Boundaries** (Strategy #30)
- Ask for what you need.
- Act to get what you need.
- Protect yourself from being hurt or taken advantage of again.
- Set internal boundaries:
  - Stop blaming your feelings on others and take ownership.
  - Start intentionally seeing circumstances from others' point of view.

Remove Toxic People, Places, and Things (Strategy #18)
- Act to move or remove people from your bus.
- Physically remove yourself from places that leave you vulnerable.
- Remove any substance or items that would be a temptation before.

Forgiveness (Strategy #37)
We will be exploring Forgiveness in much greater detail in Week 39.
- Choose to forgive others, whether they intentionally or unintentionally hurt you.
- Forgive God.
- Forgive yourself and be kind to yourself.

Victim mentality tries to convince us that people have ulterior motives and are actively trying to hurt us. In fact, if we are triggered, we could easily assign the old emotions of fear and danger from past trauma to our present circumstances.

If our present circumstances are healthy, then we can falsely accuse others and push away healthy relationships. If our present circumstances are unhealthy, then we should build healthy boundaries to protect ourselves.

Recognizing victim mentality and self-pity are skills we all need to learn. We can go to trusted sponsors, mentors, accountability partners, and friends to gain insight. We can also pray and ask God to help us separate what are old feelings versus what is happening now. Then He can tell us how He'd like us to proceed.

It is always best to make decisions when we are grounded and clear-headed. Pray and process first, rather than make emotionally-fueled decisions in the moment.

NOTES

A Note on Predators:

While victim mentality and self-pity warp our perception of others, it is also possible that we are actively the victim of a perpetrator. There ARE narcissists, manipulative sociopaths, and psychopaths who prey on others. They seek out individuals who are codependent and/or easy to manipulate—especially those with a history of abuse. (Victims of childhood abuse, especially sexual abuse, are more vulnerable to predators throughout life. We change this by processing and healing from the childhood abuse.)

In order to manipulate, perpetrators are masters at appearing kind, "loving," and charming. They perform acts of kindness to earn the trust of others. In fact, they may be too kind or too loving too fast. They move quickly in romantic relationships because perpetrators want our commitment before we recognize their true colors.

We do not have to live in fear of these kinds of people or relationships. We can proactively protect ourselves in two ways: The first is educating ourselves on the behaviors of perpetrators to help us identify them. The second is continuing our healing journey to help us become strong, healthy children of God. As we become more confident and capable, we are less and less susceptible to manipulation.

Additional Resources: *Safe People* by Dr. Cloud and Dr. Townsend

WEEKLY WORSHIP
"I Am No Victim" by Kristine DiMarco

DISCUSSION QUESTIONS

1. Have you ever considered victim mentality to be an issue for you? If not, has this lesson changed your perspective?

2. Which symptoms of self-pity in the list above can you identify with?

3. How can you use an Eternal Perspective to counteract some of the victim mentality or self-pity you are being tempted by?

NOTES

Identifying Victim Mentality Worksheet
Week 30 Homework

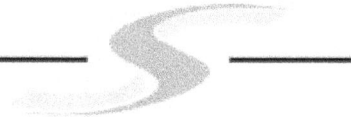

Instructions
We recommend you set aside a couple hours of uninterrupted time to work through the Freedom Process and Plan for Freedom. It's most helpful when you can do the entire homework in one sitting. If you need to pause to process or cry, we recommend doing so after the Prayer for Healing to reduce any opportunity for the enemy to distract. Get your tissues and chocolates ready. If it would be helpful for you, have worship music playing in the background. Remember, choose to read every word out loud for every prayer.

Prayer for Surrender
Father God, thank You for creating me, _____ (your name), in Your image. Thank You for designing me perfectly for Your calling on my life. As a loving Father, please show me who I am in You. Help me understand and separate the _____ (your name) You created from everything else. Help me see and understand how I've been influenced or controlled by anything other than Your Holy Spirit. I surrender **victim mentality**. Help me to identify and separate from any lies in this area that I'm still believing. Help me continue to see the _____ (your name) You created me to be without the **victim mentality**.

Symptom Chart Exercise
Review the following table and consider which symptoms you've experienced. Mark all the symptoms that apply to you. Ask the Holy Spirit to guide you.

Later, if you are confused about what you are feeling or how the enemy is attacking you, this tool will become a resource to help you sift through the lies, so you can easily identify them and eliminate them.

Victim Mentality

Emotional Symptoms

Self Pity/ Pity Parties
Feelings of inferiority or being defeated
Feeling discounted, dismissed, or disenfranchised
Hopelessness
Depression
Constant Fear
Feeling unsafe
Feeling trapped
Feeling powerless to change

Tangible Symptoms

Lack of motivation to change
Lack of fighting back
Leaving yourself vulnerable
Refusal to set boundaries
Refusal to actively fight for what you need
Having a "chip on your shoulder"
Low energy levels
Always the underdog
Continued patterns of abuse
Various Illness
Poor posture or facing down
Self-sabotaging, failing, quitting, running away
Poverty mindset

Spiritual Symptoms

Lack of hope for God's plan
Lack of faith in God's promises
Believing God's punishment is deserved
Believing God doesn't help me
Believing the enemy always attacks me
Believing God will never bless me
Perceived lack of spiritual gifts

Thought Symptoms

Self-doubt and lack of confidence
Pessimism and cynicism
Expecting to be hurt
Repeatedly choosing to give up or quit
Any criticism is received as an attack
Believing you cannot/should not ask for what you need
"Everyone is prejudiced against me."
"Nothing ever works out for me."
"It's my job to take the abuse. I deserve punishment."
"I'll never be able to do/learn that."
"The world is against me."
"This is how all relationships work."
"Everyone will end up hurting me."

Victim Mentality Questions:

1. List the circumstances and relationships where **victim mentality** has played a role in your life. *(For example: staying silent, giving up, choosing destructive or self-harming behavior, building resentments, etc.)*

2. How did a **victim mentality** play a role in your childhood?

3. Where has a **victim mentality** played a role in your relationships as an adult?

4. How has a **victim mentality** affected your decisions?

5. How has a **victim mentality** interfered with your relationship with God?

6. Are you ready to repent of a **victim mentality** and let Jesus take it? _____

Instructions

Unforgiveness can actually block your ability to get rid of lies and receive healing. Write a list of people and situations you need to forgive. Next, use the prayer template to pray through all of the people/instances on your list. Pray them through as many times as necessary to have a clear conscience on forgiveness.

Prayer of Forgiveness

Father God, thank You for shining Your light into my life to expose any unforgiveness or bitterness still hiding. Because I want Your full forgiveness as bought for me through Jesus's death on the cross, I choose to forgive those who have hurt or offended me.

I forgive _____ for _____.

I forgive You, God, for any perceived hurt or offense that I've held against you. Specifically, _____.

As I fully accept God's forgiveness, I choose to forgive myself for _____.
I accept full forgiveness in Christ.

List:

People and situations I need to forgive:

_____
_____
_____
_____
_____
_____
_____
_____
_____
_____
_____

God: _____
_____
_____
_____

Myself: _____
_____
_____
_____

Instructions

First, make a list of specific lies you have believed surrounding the **victim mentality**. Next, pray the Prayer of Repentance for each lie in your list *out loud*. Finally, pray the Prayer of Freedom for each lie in your list *out loud*.

List

To identify the specific lies you will be repenting of and getting rid of, list the variations of **victim mentality** that you've inherited or practiced: *(For example: staying silent, giving up, choosing destructive or self-harming behavior, building resentments, etc.)*

Prayer of Repentance

Father God, I come to You on behalf of myself and my generational heritage. I repent and disown all **victim mentality** that my forefathers or I have been in agreement with. I reject and turn away from **victim mentality**, including _____ (specific examples) and ask for Your forgiveness as paid for by Jesus's blood on the cross of Calvary. I accept Your complete forgiveness that casts my sins away as far as the East is from the West.

Prayer for Freedom

In the name of Jesus Christ, by the power of the Holy Spirit, I bind **victim mentality**. You will not be able to express yourself in any harmful way. I take authority over **victim mentality**, including _____ (specific examples) and command you to leave me. I do not want you to be in my life in any shape or form. I command you to leave me and go to hell. I choose God's life and truth instead. Leave now and don't ever come back. You are not welcome here. Holy Spirit, please enforce this eviction. Thank you, Father God, for total and complete freedom from the lies of **victim mentality**.

_____
_____
_____
_____
_____
_____
_____
_____
_____
_____
_____
_____
_____
_____
_____
_____
_____
_____
_____
_____
_____
_____
_____
_____
_____
_____
_____
_____
_____

Prayer for Healing

Father God, thank You so much for total and complete freedom from **victim mentality**. Father, in Your loving mercy, I ask for You to heal any damage the enemy caused in my relationship with You, myself or others due to **victim mentality**. I ask that You restore and rebuild the healthy relationships You designed for me. Help me to connect to You in a deeper way. Please heal my spirit from any damage. Please bring peace and connection to my mind, will, and emotions. Rewire my soul to remove the old ruts of **victim mentality** and create new understanding and thought patterns aligned with Your truth. Help me to celebrate myself as Your temple in a new way. Please connect my spirit, soul, and body to each other in the healthy ways You designed. Help me to reconnect and rebuild relationships with others as Yu guide me for my good and Your glory.

Father God, I ask for physical healing from any damage done by **victim mentality**. I ask that You would heal and restore damage to my DNA, cellular structures, tissues, organs, and systems. Where creative miracles are needed, please recreate. Please heal the balance of hormones and chemicals in my body to reach homeostasis. Heal my body to work in the way You designed it to work without the interference of the enemy.

Thank You for complete healing, inside and out, head to toe, spirit, soul, and body! In Jesus's name, Amen.

ADDITIONAL HEALING NEEDED: Write below the specific healings you are asking God for today (diseases, difficult circumstances, etc.). Ask God for what you need.

Congratulations!! Awesome job praying through these prayers!! You'll want to pray through them again whenever you feel this lie is gaining ground in your life. Trauma triggers and old habits may reopen the door to these lies. Don't get discouraged. Just clear them out again. If you don't have your books handy, pray whatever God gives you to repent and get rid of the lies.

Letter Exercise

Write a letter to your **victim mentality**. Explain why you don't need to believe the lie any longer and write in detail the truth you are claiming and believing instead. Once it is complete, read the letter out loud. (Do not skip this step! There is power in words!)

Plan to Fight Back
Week 30 Homework

As you move forward, the thoughts and emotions from **victim mentality** may tempt you to fall back into old patterns. It's important to have a plan to fight back so you're not caught off guard.

Review the list of strategies in the appendix. Which strategies will you use to stay free of **victim mentality**?

-
-
-
-
-
-

Next, use the **Victim Mentality** Symptom Chart found at the beginning of this homework to help create a plan to fight back.

1. Review the "Spiritual Symptoms" you marked for **victim mentality**. In the "Prayers" section of the blank chart following, write a specific statement of faith or prayer for each symptom you marked.

2. Review the "Emotional Symptoms" you marked for **victim mentality**. In the "Scriptures" section of the blank chart following, write specific scripture verses you will use as your "sword of spirit" for each emotional pattern you marked.

3. Review the "Thought Symptoms" you marked for **victim mentality**. In the "God Says" section, write a specific statement beginning with "God says…" to replace each of the thought patterns you marked.

4. Review the "Tangible Symptoms" you marked for **victim mentality**. In the "Action Steps" section, write the action steps you'll take to replace the tangible habits and behaviors you marked.

Scriptures

Action Steps

Victim Mentality

Prayers

God Says...

Accountability Share
Make sure you share with a trusted person about your freedom from **victim mentality**. Do not consider this lesson finished until you have shared. You'll be amazed at the transformative power it holds.

I will share the following:
- Answers to the processing questions
- My plan to fight back
- New revelations or understanding about my past
- Feelings or thoughts I'm still struggling to replace
- Questions of confusion I may have about the lie or the process
- Feelings of shame or guilt that are still present

I will share them with _____ (name).

Cleaning House Exercise
List any items in your possession that represent **victim mentality**.

-
-
-
-
-
-

Would you be willing to get rid of these items? What is God asking you to do?

Identifying Self-Pity Worksheet
Week 30 Homework

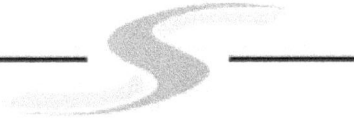

Instructions
We recommend you set aside a couple hours of uninterrupted time to work through the Freedom Process and Plan for Freedom. It's most helpful when you can do the entire homework in one sitting. If you need to pause to process or cry, we recommend doing so after the Prayer for Healing to reduce any opportunity for the enemy to distract. Get your tissues and chocolates ready. If it would be helpful for you, have worship music playing in the background. Remember, choose to read every word out loud for every prayer.

Prayer for Surrender
Father God, thank You for creating me, _____ (your name), in Your image. Thank You for designing me perfectly for Your calling on my life. As a loving Father, please show me who I am in You. Help me understand and separate the _____ (your name) You created from everything else. Help me see and understand how I've been influenced or controlled by anything other than Your Holy Spirit. I surrender **self-pity**. Help me to identify and separate from any lies in this area that I'm still believing. Help me continue to see the _____ (your name) You created me to be without the **self-pity**.

Symptom Chart Exercise
Review the following table and consider which symptoms you've experienced. Mark all the symptoms that apply to you. Ask the Holy Spirit to guide you.

Later, if you are confused about what you are feeling or how the enemy is attacking you, this tool will become a resource to help you sift through the lies, so you can easily identify them and eliminate them.

Emotional Symptoms

Resentful of those who get what they want
Feeling proud of problems or illness
Hopeless
Depression
Feeling sorry for one's self
Hyper empathy
Recurring emotional flashbacks despite treatment
Proud of unfairness or hurts
Proud of illness

Tangible Symptoms

Spiraling/Compounding thoughts and emotions
Lack of motivation to change
Sulking
False humility
Lack of fighting back
Leaving yourself vulnerable
Projecting past problems onto the future
Continued patterns of abuse
Illness, sickliness
Low energy levels
Living out Murphy's Law

Self-Pity

Spiritual Symptoms

Lack of hope for God's plan
Lack of faith in God's promises
Believing God wanted the hurt to happen "to me"
Believing God doesn't want to heal me or help me
Believing God doesn't want to protect me
Believing God wants me to be a martyr

Thought Symptoms

Thoughts stuck in the past
Focusing on everything that is bad
Blaming others for not providing what you need
Bragging about problems, illness
Comparing problems with others
Focus on things going wrong or lack
Pessimism
Believing everything happens "to me" (self-centered)
"Poor me."
"Why me?"
"It's always me."
"They made me feel this way."

Processing Questions:

1. List the circumstances and relationships where **self-pity** has played a role in your life. *(For example: wallowing or complaining to avoid changing, ignoring others' feelings, or refusing to create healthy boundaries, etc.)*

2. How did **self-pity** play a role in your childhood?

3. Where has **self-pity** played a role in your relationships as an adult?

4. How has **self-pity** affected your decisions?

5. How has **self-pity** interfered with your relationship with God?

6. Are you ready to repent of **self-pity** and let Jesus take it? _____

Instructions

Unforgiveness can actually block your ability to get rid of lies and receive healing. Write a list of people and situations you need to forgive. Next, use the prayer template to pray through all of the people/instances on your list. Pray them through as many times as necessary to have a clear conscience on forgiveness.

Prayer of Forgiveness

Father God, thank You for shining Your light into my life to expose any unforgiveness or bitterness still hiding. Because I want Your full forgiveness as bought for me through Jesus's death on the cross, I choose to forgive those who have hurt or offended me.

I forgive _____ for
_____.

I forgive You, God, for any perceived hurt or offense that I've held against you. Specifically,
_____.

As I fully accept God's forgiveness, I choose to forgive myself for _____.
I accept full forgiveness in Christ.

List:

People and situations I need to forgive:

_____

_____

_____

_____

_____

_____

_____

_____

_____

_____

_____

God: _____

_____

_____

_____

Myself: _____

_____

_____

_____

Instructions

First, make a list of specific lies you have believed surrounding the **self-pity**. Next, pray the Prayer of Repentance for each lie in your list *out loud*. Finally, pray the Prayer of Freedom for each lie in your list *out loud*.

Prayer of Repentance

Father God, I come to You on behalf of myself and my generational heritage. I repent and disown all **self-pity** that my forefathers or I have been in agreement with. I reject and turn away from **self-pity**, including _____ (specific examples) and ask for Your forgiveness as paid for by Jesus's blood on the cross of Calvary. I accept Your complete forgiveness that casts my sins away as far as the East is from the West.

Prayer for Freedom

In the name of Jesus Christ, by the power of the Holy Spirit, I bind **self-pity**. You will not be able to express yourself in any harmful way. I take authority over **self-pity** including _____ (specific examples) and command you to leave me. I do not want you to be in my life in any shape or form. I command you to leave me and go to hell. I choose God's life and truth instead. Leave now and don't ever come back. You are not welcome here. Holy Spirit, please enforce this eviction. Thank you, Father God, for total and complete freedom from the lies of **self-pity**.

List

To identify the specific lies you will be repenting of and getting rid of, list the variations of **self-pity** that you've inherited or practiced:
(For example: wallowing or complaining to avoid changing, ignoring others' feelings, or refusing to create healthy boundaries, etc.)

_____
_____
_____
_____
_____
_____
_____
_____
_____
_____
_____
_____
_____
_____
_____
_____
_____
_____
_____
_____
_____
_____
_____
_____
_____
_____
_____
_____
_____

Prayer for Healing

Father God, thank You so much for total and complete freedom from **self-pity**. Father, in Your loving mercy, I ask for You to heal any damage the enemy caused in my relationship with You, myself, or others due to **self-pity**. I ask that You restore and rebuild the healthy relationships You designed for me. Help me to connect to You in a deeper way. Please heal my spirit from any damage. Please bring peace and connection to my mind, will, and emotions. Rewire my soul to remove the old ruts of **self-pity** and create new understanding and thought patterns aligned with Your truth. Help me to celebrate myself as Your temple in a new way. Please connect my spirit, soul, and body to each other in the healthy ways You designed. Help me to reconnect and rebuild relationships with others as You guide me for my good and Your glory.

Father God, I ask for physical healing from any damage done by **self-pity**. I ask that You would heal and restore damage to my DNA, cellular structures, tissues, organs, and systems. Where creative miracles are needed, please recreate. Please heal the balance of hormones and chemicals in my body to reach homeostasis. Heal my body to work in the way You designed it to work without the interference of the enemy.

Thank You for complete healing, inside and out, head to toe, spirit, soul, and body! In Jesus's name, Amen.

ADDITIONAL HEALING NEEDED: Write below the specific healings you are asking God for today (diseases, difficult circumstances, etc.). Ask God for what you need.

Congratulations!! Awesome job praying through these prayers!! You'll want to pray through them again whenever you feel this lie is gaining ground in your life. Trauma triggers and old habits may reopen the door to these lies. Don't get discouraged. Just clear them out again. If you don't have your books handy, pray whatever God gives you to repent and get rid of the lies.

Letter Exercise

Write a letter to your **self-pity**. Explain why you don't need to believe the lie any longer and write in detail the truth you are claiming and believing instead. Once it is complete, read the letter out loud. (Do not skip this step! There is power in words!)

Plan to Fight Back
Week 30 Homework

As you move forward, the thoughts and emotions from **self-pity** may tempt you to fall back into old patterns. It's important to have a plan to fight back so you're not caught off guard.

Review the list of strategies in the appendix. Which strategies will you use to stay free of **self-pity**?

-
-
-
-
-
-

Next, use the **Self-Pity** Symptom Chart found at the beginning of this homework to help create a plan to fight back.

1. Review the "Spiritual Symptoms" you marked for **self-pity**. In the "Prayers" section of the blank chart following, write a specific statement of faith or prayer for each symptom you marked.

2. Review the "Emotional Symptoms" you marked for **self-pity**. In the "Scriptures" section of the blank chart following, write specific scripture verses you will use as your "sword of spirit" for each emotional pattern you marked.

3. Review the "Thought Symptoms" you marked for **self-pity**. In the "God Says" section, write a specific statement beginning with "God says…" to replace each of the thought patterns you marked.

4. Review the "Tangible Symptoms" you marked for **self-pity**. In the "Action Steps" section, write the action steps you'll take to replace the tangible habits and behaviors you marked.

Scriptures

Action Steps

Self-Pity

Prayers

God Says...

NOTES

Accountability Share
Make sure you share with a trusted person about your freedom from **self-pity**. Do not consider this lesson finished until you have shared. You'll be amazed at the transformative power it holds.

I will share the following:
- Answers to the processing questions
- My plan to fight back
- New revelations or understanding about my past
- Feelings or thoughts I'm still struggling to replace
- Questions of confusion I may have about the lie or the process
- Feelings of shame or guilt that are still present

I will share them with _____ (name).

Cleaning House Exercise
List any items in your possession that represent **self-pity**.

-
-
-
-
-
-

Would you be willing to get rid of these items? What is God asking you to do?

Unit 3 (Part A) Assessment

1. Have you felt more capable of facing this freedom process after binding shame, guilt, and fear?

2. Did you notice anything new in your story when doing the timeline assignment?

3. What did you learn about yourself through the "Full Family Tree" exercise?

4. Did you realize more about how trauma triggers, flashbacks, and/or dissociation have played a role in your story? Explain.

5. How did it feel to reach out to your support system for help with this process?

6. What changes did you notice in your life after identifying and getting rid of the lies attached to cultural influences?

7. What changes did you notice in your life after identifying and getting rid of the lies attached to passiveness and passive aggressiveness?

8. What changes did you notice in your life after identifying and getting rid of the lies attached to denial and lying?

9. What changes did you notice in your life after identifying and getting rid of the lies attached to victim mentality?

10. What changes did you notice in your life after identifying and getting rid of the lies attached to self-pity?

Appendices

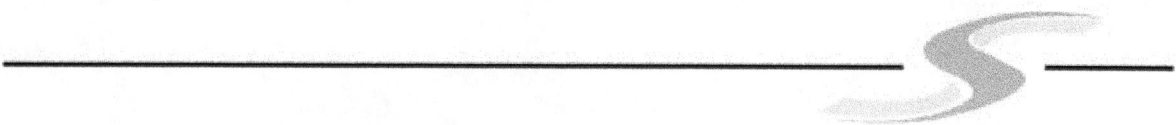

Appendix A: Who We Are Scripture List

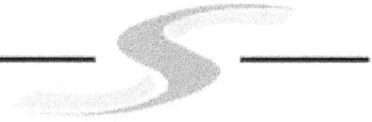

I am His friend. (John 15:15)

I am chosen. (John 15:16)

I am complete in Him. (Colossians 2:10)

I am fearfully and wonderfully made. (Psalm 139:14)

I am a new creation. (2 Corinthians 5:17)

I am His workmanship. (Ephesians 2:10)

I am light. (I Thessalonians 5:5)

I am a child of the Most High! (John 1:12, 1 John 4:4)

I am an heir of God and a joint heir with Christ. (Romans 8:17)

I am more than a conqueror. (Romans 8:37)

I am adopted as God's sons and daughters through Jesus Christ. (Ephesians 1:5)

My body is the temple of the Holy Spirit. (1 Corinthians 6:19)

I am the head and not the tail, I am at the top and never the bottom. (Deuteronomy 28:13)

I am accepted in the Beloved. (Ephesians 1:6)

I am a royal priesthood (1 Peter 2:9)

I am set apart. (Psalm 4:3)

I am totally and completely forgiven. (1 John 1:9)

I am God's intentional and perfectly planned creation. (Psalm 139:13)

Appendix B: Who God Is Scripture List

God is:

Accepting - Romans 15:7
Available - Jeremiah 29:13
Caring - 1 Peter 5:7
Close - Psalm 34:18-19
Comforter - 2 Corinthians 1:3-4
Compassionate - Lamentations 3:22-23
Deliverer - Psalm 18:2
Encouraging - Romans 15:4
Faithful - 1 Thessalonians 5:24
Father - Galatians 4:6
Forgiving - Daniel 9:9
Generous - James 1:17
Giving - John 3:16
Good - Psalm 106:1
Gracious - Ephesians 2:8-9
Healer - Psalm 103:3
Humble - Matthew 11:28-30
Light - Ephesians 5:8
Lord - Acts 10:36
Love - 1 John 4:16
Loyal - Deuteronomy 31:6
Merciful - Psalm 86:15
Mighty - Psalm 24:8
Miracle-worker - Hebrews 2:4

Omnipresent - Psalm 139:7-10
Omniscient - Psalm 139:16
Patient - 2 Peter 3:15
Powerful - Joshua 4:24
Redeemer - Isaiah 34:5
Refreshing - Acts 3:19-20
Refuge - Psalm 46:1, Psalm 91
Restorer - Psalm 23:3
Reviver - Psalm 19:7
Righteous - Psalm 89:14
Rock - Deuteronomy 32:4
Servant - Mark 10:45
Shepherd - Psalm 23:1
Shield - Proverbs 30:5
Sovereign - Daniel 5:21b
Sympathetic - Hebrews 4:15-16
Teacher - Isaiah 28:26
Transformer - 2 Corinthians 5:17
Trustworthy - Deuteronomy 7:9
Truth - John 14:6
Unchangeable - Malachi 3:6
Understanding - Isaiah 40:28
Warrior - Exodus 14:14
Wise - Job 12:13

Appendix C: Armor of God Scripture

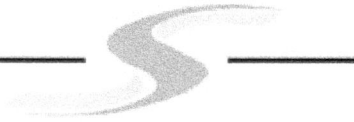

Ephesians 6:10-18 (NKJV)

"Finally, my brethren, be strong in the Lord and in the power of His might. Put on the whole armor of God, that you may be able to stand against the wiles of the devil. For we do not wrestle against flesh and blood, but against principalities, against powers, against the rulers of the darkness of this age, against spiritual *hosts* of wickedness in the heavenly *places*. Therefore take up the whole armor of God, that you may be able to withstand in the evil day, and having done all, to stand.

Stand therefore, having girded your waist with truth, having put on the breastplate of righteousness, and having shod your feet with the preparation of the gospel of peace; above all, taking the shield of faith with which you will be able to quench all the fiery darts of the wicked one. And take the helmet of salvation, and the sword of the Spirit, which is the word of God; praying always with all prayer and supplication in the Spirit, being watchful to this end with all perseverance and supplication for all the saints."

Download the audio version at: https://bloominthedark.org/rs4l/armor-of-god

Appendix D: The Serenity Prayer

By Reinhold Niebuhr

God,
Grant me the serenity to accept
the things I cannot change,
Courage to change the things I can,
and the Wisdom to know the difference,
Living one day at a time,
Enjoying one moment at a time,
Accepting hardship as a pathway to peace,
Taking, as Jesus did,
This sinful world as it is,
Not as I would have it,
Trusting that You will make all things right,
If I surrender to Your will,
So that I may be reasonably happy in this life,
And supremely happy with You forever in the next.
Amen.

Appendix E: Worship Playlist

Lesson Name	Song	Artist
What to Expect	"Freedom Hymn"	Austin French
Saying Hello to Reality	"No Longer Slave"	Bethel
Fantasy vs Reality	"We Believe"	Newsboys
Who God Is	"Who You Say I Am"	Hillsong
God's Heart for Restoration	"Mended"	Matthew West
The Love of Father God	"Fierce"	Jesus Culture
Surrender to God	"I Surrender"	Hillsong
Positive Coping Tools	"Tremble - Live"	Mosaic MSC
Progression of Sin	"God I Look To You"	Bethel
Cognitive Distortions	"You Say"	Lauren Daigle
You Are NOT Your Emotions	"God Help Me"	Plumb
The Fullness of the Holy Spirit	"Holy Spirit You Are Welcome Here"	Francesca Battistelli
8 Steps to Freedom	"Chain Breaker"	Zach Williams
Good Grief	"We Believe"	Newsboys
Damaging Pain vs. Healing Pain	"The Hurt & The Healer"	MercyMe
Trauma Points and Symptoms	"Gracefully Broken"	Tasha Cobbs
The Real Me	"Known"	Tauren Wells
Eternal Perspective	"Build Your Kingdom Here"	Rend Collective
What Motivates You?	"Lord, I Need You"	Matt Maher
Healthy Boundaries	"Boundary Lines"	Chris Tomlin
CLearning to Stabilize	"Eye of the Storm"	Ryan Stevenson
That's Not Me	"Run Devil Run"	Crowder

Lesson Name	Song	Artist
Shame OFF You	"No Shame"	Moriah Peters
Discovering the Root	"The Voice of Truth"	Casting Crowns
Eliminating the Root	"Waging War"	Cece Winans
Diving Deep	"Way Maker"	Michael W. Smith
Uncover	"Believer"	Rhett Walker
Cultural Influences	"Slow Fade"	Casting Crowns
Passing the Buck	"Starts With Me"	Tim Timmons
Victim Mentality	"I Am No Victim"	Kristine DiMarco

Appendix F: Steps to Freedom Worksheet

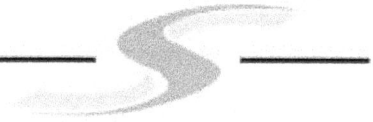

Step 1: Identify

Step 2: Take Responsibility

Step 3: Repent for Participating in the Lie

Step 4: Disown the Lie

Step 5: Get Rid of the Lie

Step 6: Fight Back

Step 7: Celebrate

Step 8: Testify and Disciple

Appendix G: Discovering the Root Worksheet

	Cause	Leads to	Becomes	Consequence
Body	Victimizing event	Unhealthy coping	Addiction	Disease, jail, death
Soul	Lie or thought filter	Belief/viewpoint	Character defect	Damaged relationships
Spirit	Spiritual door point	Lies influence behaviors	Locked into habit of lies	Separation from God

Appendix H: Identifying Trauma & Triggers Worksheet

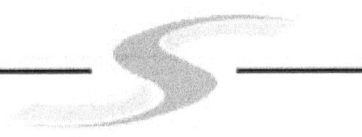

Before filling out the chart below, get into a safe place where you will not be interrupted or disturbed. Have your list of promises handy and ready to fight lies or triggers if they arise.

Trigger/Trauma	Intensity (1-10)	Response or Feelings	Truth that stabilizes
Getting yelled at	7	fear, shame, hiding	"I am not responsible for other's reactions. I do not deserve to get yelled at. I don't need to be afraid."

Appendix I: Peeling The Onion

Consider the image of the spiral below. Notice how the lies get closer and closer to the center, similar to an onion. The lies on the outside of the spiral have marginal impact on our lives alone. But as we get closer to the center, the lies begin to affect us more and more deeply. The lies in our minds can be louder and seem more important. The feelings we experience as a result of these lies get more and more intense as we press on.

We start on the outside of spiral for two reasons: first, because these are the easiest to uncover and eliminate and, second, because we'll need to build our identifying skills and muscles before we can tackle the more deeply set lies.

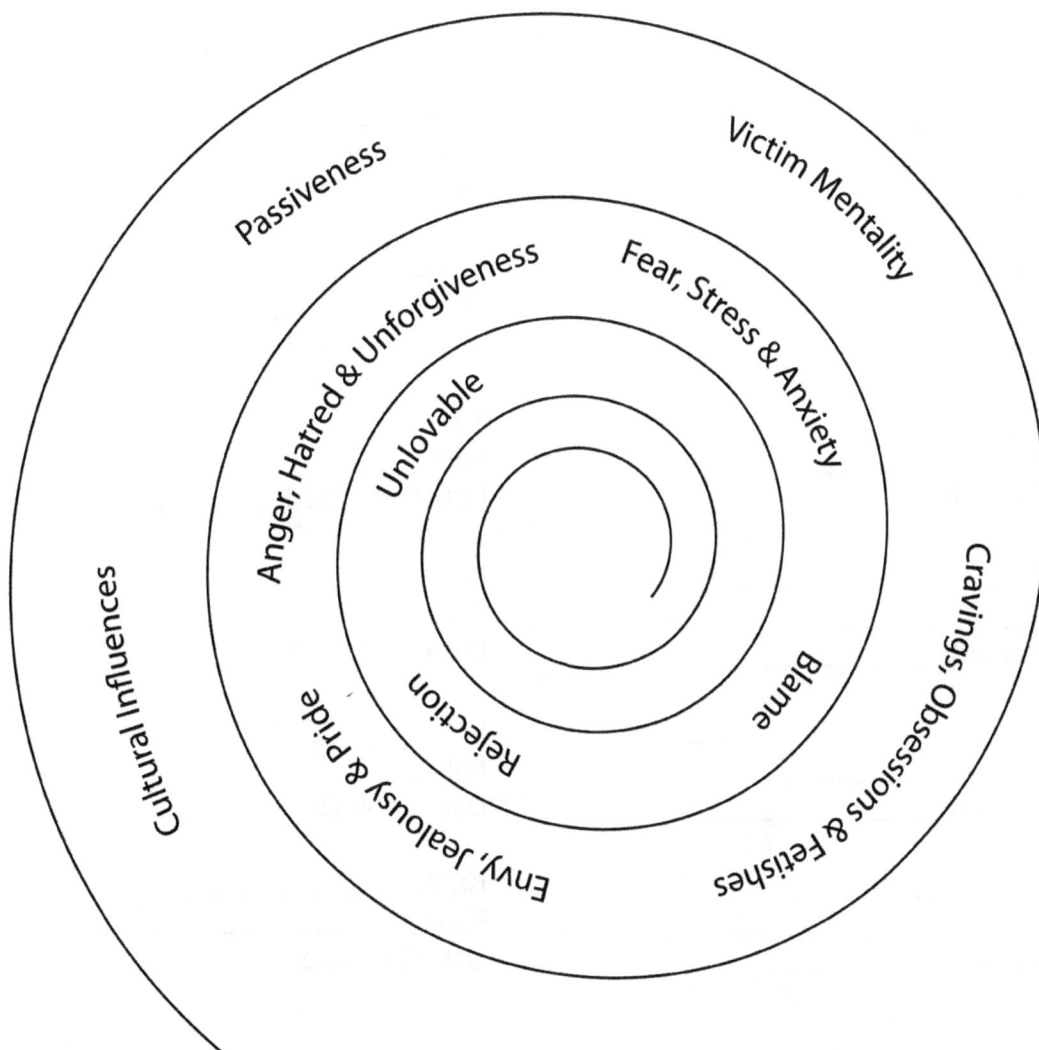

Appendix J: Reach Out to Support System

Reach out to your support system:

Optional Script:
"Thank you so much for being part of my healing journey. In the next three months, I will be addressing the spiritual roots of a lot of the damage in my life and family of origin. This will be an intense time of getting rid of lies that have trapped me in the damage of my past. Would you be willing to walk this part of my journey with me? The enemy doesn't like losing ground, so stuff will get more intense as I kick his lies out of my life. I will need extra prayers, extra support, and extra reminders of truth. I may need to share stuff from my past that will be tough to be honest about. I don't need judgment or challenging questions. I just need love, acceptance and support during this time. Even if you don't understand the process, please just show me God's unconditional love. Can you commit to helping me?"

Name: _____
Role: _____
Date Contacted: _____

Name: _____
Role: _____
Date Contacted: _____

Name: _____
Role: _____
Date Contacted: _____

Name: _____
Role: _____
Date Contacted: _____

Name: _____
Role: _____
Date Contacted: _____

Name: _____
Role: _____
Date Contacted: _____

Name: _____
Role: _____
Date Contacted: _____

Name: _____
Role: _____
Date Contacted: _____

Name: _____
Role: _____
Date Contacted: _____

Name: _____
Role: _____
Date Contacted: _____

Name: _____
Role: _____
Date Contacted: _____

Name: _____
Role: _____
Date Contacted: _____

Appendix K: Prayer to Break Generational Curses

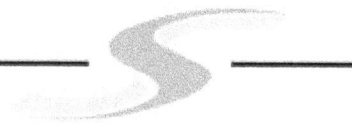

Pray through this prayer for each of the lies, sins, or curses that you listed above. Believe that God will honor your sincere repentance, forgive you, and break the curses caused by you and your previous generations.

Heavenly Father,
On my behalf and on behalf of the generations before me, I repent for believing the lie of
_____ (describe or name the lie). I make no agreement with these lies. Let the consequences of my forefathers' sins be broken along my family tree. I choose to separate myself from those lies and change my heart and actions here today. I ask Your forgiveness on their behalf and on behalf of myself and my children. Through the blood of Jesus, I receive Your forgiveness. Thank You for the opportunity to come back into alignment with You. I ask for all the healing—spirit, soul, and body—that comes with that alignment. Continue to open my eyes to any unidentified generational sin, lies, and curses so I can choose repentance and freedom. In the name of Jesus Christ of Nazareth and by the power of the Holy Spirit, let this be done on earth as it is in heaven. Amen.

Appendix L: Sample of Freedom Process

Instructions
This is a sample of the process you will be going through for every category of lies we will address in the next three months. Please read it and get familiar with the concepts included. You may want to read it **out loud** since that will be what you will be doing for each prayer in each lesson for the rest of this unit. This process may feel repetitive or unnecessary, but there is power in our words. We bind and loose things in heaven and on earth with the spoken word. Choose to read every word out loud for every prayer the first time through each lesson. After that, when you're continuing to get rid of the same lies again as you continue to choose freedom, feel free to use your own words. There is no "magical power" in these specific words, but there is power in the concepts these words represent.

Prayer for Surrender
Father God, thank You for creating me, _____ (your name), in Your image. Thank You for designing me perfectly for Your calling on my life. As a loving Father, please show me who I am in You. Help me understand and separate the _____ (your name) You created from everything else. Help me see and understand how I've been influenced or controlled by anything other than Your Holy Spirit. I surrender my _____ (lie). Help me to identify and separate from any lies in this area that I'm still believing. Help me continue to see the _____ (your name) You created me to be without the _____ (lie). Amen.

Symptom Chart Exercise
Review the following table and consider which symptoms you've experienced. Mark all the symptoms that apply to you. Ask the Holy Spirit to guide you.

Later, if you are confused about what you are feeling or how the enemy is attacking you, this tool will become a resource to help you sift through the lies, so you can easily identify them and eliminate them.

Emotional Symptoms

Sample Symptom
Sample Symptom
Sample Symptom
Sample Symptom

Tangible Symptoms

Sample Symptom
Sample Symptom
Sample Symptom
Sample Symptom

Sample Lie

Spiritual Symptoms

Sample Symptom
Sample Symptom
Sample Symptom
Sample Symptom

Thought Symptoms

Sample Symptom
Sample Symptom
Sample Symptom
Sample Symptom

Processing Questions:

1. List the circumstances and relationships where _____ (lie) has played a role in your life. *(For example: ... etc.)*

2. How did _____ (lie) play a role in your childhood?

3. Where has _____ (lie) played a role in your relationships as an adult?

4. How has _____ (lie) affected your decisions?

5. How has _____ (lie) interfered with your relationship with God?

6. Are you ready to repent of _____ (lie) and let Jesus take it? _____

Instructions
Unforgiveness can actually block your ability to get rid of lies and receive healing. Write a list of people and situations you need to forgive. Next, use the prayer template to pray through all of the people/instances on your list. Pray them through as many times as necessary to have a clear conscience on forgiveness.

Prayer of Forgiveness
Father God, thank You for shining Your light into my life to expose any unforgiveness or bitterness still hiding. Because I want Your full forgiveness as bought for me through Jesus's death on the cross, I choose to forgive those who have hurt or offended me.

I forgive _____ for
_____.

I forgive You, God, for any perceived hurt or offense that I've held against you. Specifically, _____.

As I fully accept God's forgiveness, I choose to forgive myself for _____.
I accept full forgiveness in Christ.

List:
People and situations I need to forgive:
_____
_____
_____
_____
_____
_____
_____
_____
_____
_____
_____

God: _____
_____
_____
_____

Myself: _____
_____
_____
_____

Instructions
First, make a list of specific lies you have believed surrounding the _____ (lie). Next, pray the Prayer of Repentance for each lie in your list **out loud**. Finally, pray the Prayer of Freedom for each lie in your list **out loud**.

List:
To identify the specific lies you will be repenting of and getting rid of, list the variations of _____ (lie) that you've inherited or practiced: (*For example: ...*)

_____
_____
_____
_____
_____
_____
_____
_____
_____
_____
_____
_____
_____

Prayer of Repentance
Father God, I come to You on behalf of myself and my generational heritage. I repent and disown all _____ (lie) that my forefathers or I have been in agreement with. I reject and turn away from _____ (lie), including _____ (specific examples) and ask for Your forgiveness as paid for by Jesus's blood on the cross of Calvary. I accept Your complete forgiveness that casts my sins away as far as the East is from the West.

_____
_____
_____
_____
_____
_____
_____

Prayer for Freedom
In the name of Jesus Christ, by the power of the Holy Spirit, I bind _____ (lie). You will not be able to express yourself in any harmful way. I take authority over _____ (lie), including _____ (specific examples) and command you to leave me. I do not want you to be in my life in any shape or form. I command you to leave me and go to hell. I choose God's life and truth instead. Leave now and don't ever come back. You are not welcome here. Holy Spirit, please enforce this eviction. Thank you, Father God, for total and complete freedom

_____
_____
_____
_____
_____
_____
_____
_____
_____
_____
_____
_____
_____

Prayer for Healing

Father God, thank You so much for total and complete freedom from _____ (lie). Father, in Your loving mercy, I ask for You to heal any damage the enemy caused in my relationship with You, myself or others due to _____ (lie). I ask that You restore and rebuild the healthy relationships You designed for me. Help me to connect to You in a deeper way. Please heal my spirit from any damage. Please bring peace and connection to my mind, will and emotions. Rewire my soul to remove the old ruts of _____ (lie) and create new understanding and thought patterns aligned with Your truth.

Help me to celebrate myself as Your temple in a new way. Please connect my spirit, soul, and body to each other in the healthy ways You designed. Help me to reconnect and rebuild relationships with others as You guide me for my good and Your glory.

Father God, I ask for physical healing from any damage done by _____ (lie). I ask that You would heal and restore damage to my DNA, cellular structures, tissues, organs, and systems. Where creative miracles are needed, please recreate. Please heal the balance of hormones and chemicals in my body to reach homeostasis. Heal my body to work in the way You designed it to work without the interference of the enemy.

Thank You for complete healing, inside and out, head to toe, spirit, soul, and body! In Jesus's name, Amen.

ADDITIONAL HEALING NEEDED: Write below the specific healings you are asking God for today (diseases, difficult circumstances, etc.). Ask God for what you need.

Congratulations!! Awesome job praying through these prayers!! You'll want to pray through them again whenever you feel this lie is gaining ground in your life. Trauma triggers and old habits may reopen the door to these lies. Don't get discouraged. Just clear them out again. If you don't have your books handy, pray whatever God gives you to repent and get rid of the lies.

Letter Exercise

Write a letter to your _____ (lie). Explain why you don't need to believe the lie any longer and write in detail the truth you are claiming and believing instead. Once it is complete, read the letter out loud. (Do not skip this step! There is power in words!)

Appendix M: Sample Plan to Fight Back

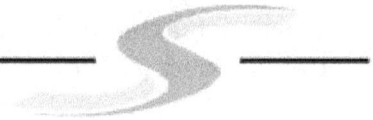

As you move forward, the thoughts and emotions from _____ (lie) may tempt you to fall back into old patterns. It's important to have a plan to fight back so you're not caught off guard.

Review the list of strategies in the appendix. Which strategies will you use to stay free of _____ (lie)?

-
-
-
-
-
-

Next, use the _____ (lie) Symptom Chart found at the beginning of this homework to help create a plan to fight back.

1. Review the "Spiritual Symptoms" you marked for _____ (lie). In the "Prayers" section of the blank chart following, write a specific statement of faith or prayer for each symptom you marked.

2. Review the "Emotional Symptoms" you marked for _____ (lie). In the "Scriptures" section of the blank chart following, write specific scripture verses you will use as your "sword of spirit" for each emotional pattern you marked.

3. Review the "Thought Symptoms" you marked for _____ (lie). In the "God Says" section, write a specific statement beginning with "God says…" to replace each of the thought patterns you marked.

4. Review the "Tangible Symptoms" you marked for _____ (lie). In the "Action Steps" section, write the action steps you'll take to replace the tangible habits and behaviors you marked.

Scriptures

Action Steps

Plan To Fight
Sample

Prayers

God Says...

NOTES

Accountability Share
Make sure you share with a trusted person about your freedom from _____ (lie). Do not consider this lesson finished until you have shared. You'll be amazed at the transformative power it holds.

I will share the following:
- Answers to the processing questions
- My plan to fight back
- New revelations or understanding about my past
- Feelings or thoughts I'm still struggling to replace
- Questions of confusion I may have about the lie or the process
- Feelings of shame or guilt that are still present

I will share them with _____ (name).

Cleaning House Exercise
List any items in your possession that represent _____ (lie).

-
-
-
-
-
-

Would you be willing to get rid of these items? What is God asking you to do?

Appendix N: Hotlines

General Christian Counseling Services
New Life Clinics: 1-800-NEW-LIFE
National Prayer Line: 1-800-4-PRAYER
Liberty Godparent Ministry: 1-800-368-3336
Grace Help Line 24 Hour Christian Service: 1-800-982-8032
The 700 Club Hotline: 1-800-759-0700
Want to Know Jesus?: 1-800-NEED-HIM
Biblical Help for Youth in Crisis: 1-800-HIT-HOME
Rapha National Network: 1-800-383-HOPE
Emerge Ministries: 330-867-5603
Association of Christian Counselors: 1-800-526-8673

Abortion
National Abortion Federation Hotline: 1-800-772-9100
Post Abortion Counseling: 1-800-228-0332
Post Abortion Project Rachel: 1-800-5WE-CARE

Abuse
National Sexual Assault Hotline: 1-800-656-HOPE (4673)
Stop It Now!: 1-888-PREVENT
United States Elder Abuse Hotline: 1-866-363-4276
Child Abuse Hotline/Dept. of Social Services: 1-800-342-3720
Missing Children Help Center: 1-800-872-5437

Addiction
Families Anonymous: 1-800-736-9805
Drug Abuse National Helpline: 1-800-662-4357
National Assoc. for Children of Alcoholics: 1-888-554-2627
Alcoholics for Christ: 1-800-441-7877

Cancer
American Cancer Society: 1-800-227-2345
National Cancer institute: 1-800-422-6237

Caregivers
Elder Care Locator: 1-800-677-1116
Well Spouse Foundation: 1-800-838-0879

Chronic Illness/Chronic Pain
Rest Ministries: 1-888-751-REST (7378)

Crisis Numbers for Teens (Under 18)
Girls and Boys Town: 1-800-448-3000
Youth Crisis Hotline: 1-800-448-4663

Crisis Pregnancy Helpline
Crisis Pregnancy Hotline: 1-800-67-BABY-6
Liberty Godparent Ministry: 1-800-368-3336

Cult Information
Cult Hotline (Mercy House): 606-748-9961

Domestic Violence
National Domestic Violence Hotline: 1-800-799-SAFE
National Domestic Violence Hotline (Spanish): 1-800-942-6908
Battered Women and their Children: 1-800-603-HELP
RAINN: 1-800-656-HOPE (4673)

Eating Disorders
Eating Disorders Awareness and Prevention: 1-800-931-2237
Eating Disorders Center: 1-888-236-1188
National Association of Anorexia Nervosa and Associated Disorders: 1-847-831-3438

Family Violence
Family Violence Prevention Center: 1-800-313-1310

Gambling
Compulsive Gambling Hotline: 410-332-0402

Grief/Loss
GriefShare: 1-800-395-5755

Homeless/Shelters
Homeless: 1-800-231-6946
American Family Housing: 1-888-600-4357

Homosexual/Lesbian
Recovery: Exodus International: 1-888-264-0877
Gay and Lesbian National Hotline: 1-888-843-4564
Trevor Hotline (Suicide): 1-866-4-U-TREVOR

Parents
Building Futures: 1-800-A-WAY-OUT
United States Missing Children Hotline: 1-800-235-3535

Rape/Sexual Assault
RAINN: 1-800-656-HOPE (4673)

Runaways
Covenant House Nineline: 1-800-999-9999
National Runaway Switchboard: 1-800-621-4000
Youth Crisis Hotline: 1-800-448-4663

Self-Injury, "Cutting"
S.A.F.E. (Self Abuse Finally Ends): 1-800-DONT-CUT

Sexual Addiction
Focus on the Family: 1-800-A-FAMILY

Suicide
Suicide Hotline: 1-800-273-TALK (8255)
Suicide Prevention Hotline: 1-800-827-7571
Deaf Hotline: 1-800-799-4TTY
NineLine: 1-800-999-9999
Holy Spirit Teenline: 1-800-722-5385
Crisis Intervention: 1-800-673-2496

Appendix O: Additional Resources

The content, information, opinions, and viewpoints contained in these additional resources are solely those of the authors or contributors of such materials. We are not endorsing the authors below, nor have they necessarily endorsed the RS4L course. The books are intended for general informational purposes only.

A More Excellent Way, Dr. Henry Wright

Armor of God Bible Study, Priscilla Shirer

Battlefield of the Mind, Joyce Meyers

Boundaries, Dr. Townsend & Dr. Cloud

Bloom In The Dark: True Stories of Hope and Redemption, Paula Mosher Wallace

Bloom Forward: A Journal to Renew Your Mind, Wallace, Snow, Priz

The Body Keeps The Score, Bessel Van der Kolk, MD

Captivating, John & Stacey Eldridge

Crazy Love, Francis Chan

Ditch The Drama, Ginny Priz

Do You Know Who I Am, Angela Thomas

Emotions, Dr. Charles Stanley

Unashamed, Christine Caine

Uninvited, Lysa Terkeurst

Walking with God, John Eldridge

Appendix P: RS4L Strategies

Unit 1: Relationship With God

	Lesson Title	Strategy
Week 1	What To Expect	#1 – Be Honest With Yourself
		#2 – Recovery is a Journey Not a Destination
		#3 – Baby Steps
Week 2	Saying Hello to Reality	#4 – Healthy Support System
		#5 – Make Changes to Face Reality
Week 3	Fantasy vs Reality	#6 – Grace for Realistic Recovery
		#7 – Progress Not Perfection
Week 4	Who God Is	#8 – Understanding Your Intrinsic Value
Week 5	God's Heart for Restoration	#9 – God Can Restore As If Never Broken
Week 7	Surrender to God	#10 – Putting on the Armor of God
		#11 – Worship
Week 8	Positive Coping Tools	#12 – Emotional Scheduling
		#13 – Prayer & Meditation
		#14 – Gratitude
		#15 – Bilateral Processing
		#16 – Self-Care
Week 9	Progression of Sin	#17 – Taking Thoughts Captive
Week 11	You are NOT your Emotions	#18 – Remove Toxic People, Place, Things
		#19 – Emotional Detox

Unit 2: Healing Strategies

Week 12	Fullness of the Holy Spirit	#20 – Fullness of the Holy Spirit
Week 14	Good GRIEF!	#21 – Healthy Grieving
Week 15	Damaging Pain vs Healing Pain	#22 – Physical Release
Week 17	The Real Me	#23 – Who Am I? #24 – Recognizing & Replacing Lies
Week 18	Eternal Perspective	#25 – Eternal Perspective #26 – Tree of Life versus Death
Week 19	What Motivates You?	#27 – Motivation #28 – Scripture #29 – Obedience
Week 20	Healthy Boundaries	#30 – Healthy Boundaries #31 – Whose Opinion Matters
Week 21	Learning to Stabilize	#32 – Grounding #33 - Processing

Unit 3: Healing From The Past

Week 26	Diving Deep	#34 – Identifying Triggers #35 – Identifying Flashbacks #36 – Identifying Dissociation

Unit 4: Claiming Your Freedom

Week 39	Unfair Grace	#37 - Forgiveness
Week 42	Get Into The Ring	#38 – Facing Your Goliath
Week 45	Celebrate	#39 - Celebrating

Unit 5: Walking In Freedom

Appendix Q: Listening Guide Answer Keys

Week 23: Shame OFF You

Truth #1: God created us without **SHAME.**

Truth #2: Jesus **DESPISED** the shame and dealt with it for us.

Truth #3: We can be **WITHOUT** shame.

Week 24: Discovering the Root

Truth #1: There is a **PROGRESSION** from cause to consequence in your spirit, soul, and body.

Truth #2: We can **IDENTIFY** the root lie.

Truth #3: Change requires owning our **PARTICIPATION** with the lie.

Week 25: Eliminating the Root

Week 26: Diving Deep

Strategy #34: Identifying **TRIGGERS**

Strategy #35: Identifying **FLASHBACKS**

Strategy #36: Identifying **DISSOCIATION**

Week 27: Uncover

Concept #1: Utilize your healthy **SUPPORT SYSTEM.**

Concept #2: Utilize your **STRATEGIES.**

Concept #3: Utilize your **RESOURCES.**

Concept #4: Utilize your **TOOLS.**

Week 28: Cultural Influences

Week 29: Passing the Buck

Week 30: Victim Mentality

BLOOM
In the dark

Using the fertilizer of our past to bloom!

Have you ever experienced a hurt so deep that it didn't qualify for a sympathy card? Did embarrassment or shame keep you from getting help or support? Do you have a loved one who's been abused?

Many women face trauma and abuse. But that doesn't have to be the end of the story. Countless women have healed from their past with God's power.

Every success story has one thing in common – hope!

We at Bloom In The Dark have seen the power of story provide the kind of hope that change lives!

Mission:

We are a 501c3 charity seeking to raise awareness about the damage caused by secret pain and abuse, and demonstrate the hope and healing found in Christ Jesus through ex-victim testimonies, connections, and tools.

Vision:

To create a culture where people choose redemption and healing in Christ Jesus so they bloom despite darkness and pain.

Values:

- LOVE: Love God, Love yourself so you can Love your neighbor
- HONESTY: Be honest with God, yourself and others especially when it hurts
- FORGIVENESS: Forgive God, yourself and others quickly
- ENCOURAGEMENT: Encourage yourself with God's Word, your words, and other's words through what you see, hear, and speak.

Learn More:

https://bloominthedark.org

Bloom Broadcasting distributes curated, Christ-centered content on IP television, IP radio and podcast platforms to share hope and healing with hurting individuals around the world.

BLOOM PODCASTS

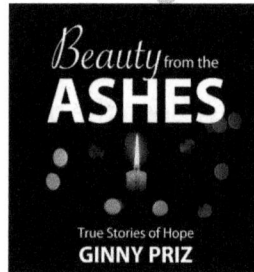

We all struggle with this broken world. Now there's content available in one place that focuses solely on healing from brokenness, abuse and addictions.

Now available on...

Available on the App Store

GET IT ON Google Play

ROKU tv amazon fireTV

Look inside

BLOOM-U
Training Center

A collection of Christian courses designed to bring hope and healing to anyone coming out of pain, abuse, or addictions.

bloom-u.org

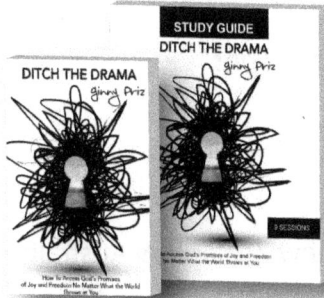

DITCH THE DRAMA

Drama creates chaos and leaves us feeling trapped in unhealthy relatonships. But it doesn't have to rule our lives or keep us stuck.

In this video Bible study you'll learn how a relationship with God can help you navigate painful emotions. Learn to experience joy and freedom no matter what kind of drama.

Beauty from the ASHES
Tools & Testimonies of Hope in Crises

THE TRUST CHALLENGE
change your perspective

Trust Academy
90 Days to Find Your Confidence

You Are Priceless
BOOT CAMP

RS4L
RECOVERY STRATEGIES 4 LIFE
Healing for your Spirit, Soul, and Body

Do you struggle with

- ☑ PTSD - Complex Trauma
- ☑ Any type of Abuse
- ☑ Addictions
- ☑ Loss
- ☑ Depression
- ☑ Fear - Stress - Anxiety
- ☑ Codependency
- ☑ Plateaued recovery

Watch Bloom Today TV Around the World

Using the fertilizer of our past to bloom today!

Ephesians 5:8-13 (NIV)
"For you were once darkness, but now you are light in the Lord. Live as children of light (for the fruit of the light consists in all goodness, righteousness and truth) and find out what pleases the Lord. Have nothing to do with the fruitless deeds of darkness, but rather expose them. It is shameful even to mention what the disobedient do in secret. But everything exposed by the light becomes visible—and everything that is illuminated becomes a light."

Television:
(Check your local listings)

Inspiration TV - INI (UK, Europe, Africa, Asia, The Caribbean, New Zealand, & Australia)
Faith USA (USA)
NRB TV (USA)
Upliftv (USA)
CTN (USA)
Alpha Omega (Romania, Moldova)
Grace Television (India)
Australia Christian Channel (Australia)
Family 7 (The Netherlands)
Flow Africa (Kwesé Channel, Africa)
Faith Africa (South Africa)
Faith Terrestrial (Eastern Cape South Africa)
Faith UK (UK)
WHTN (Middle TN)
Sacramento Faith TV (Sacramento, CA)

Online Streaming:

Amazon Prime
Parables
Inspiration TV App
Faith Broadcasting Network App

Global 7 App
Damascus Roads
NRB TV App
Grace TV App

Podcast:
iTunes
iHeartRadio
YouTube
Spreaker
Sonos

Learn More:

https://bloomtodaytv.com

Additional Resources from

BLOOM
Publishing

Find healing resources, crisis resources, and download your FREE copy of

BLOOM
in the dark

at

Bloominthedark.org/free-book

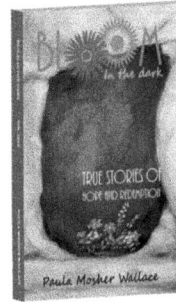

by
Paula Mosher Wallace
President of Bloom In The Dark, Inc.
paula@bloominthedark.com

A journal to renew your mind...
one day at a time.

Use this 90-day devotional journal with assessments and daily questions will help you build new thought patterns, muscle memories, and neural pathways.

BLOOM
Forward

Videos & Coaching Tools
by
Ginny Priz & Paula Mosher Wallace
Based on the Bloom Today TV show

BloomTodayTV.com

BLOOM
TODAY
WORKBOOK